# Selected Sacred Music

RECENT RESEARCHES IN MUSIC

A-R Editions publishes seven series of critical editions, spanning the history of Western music, American music, and oral traditions.

RECENT RESEARCHES IN THE MUSIC OF THE MIDDLE AGES AND EARLY RENAISSANCE
    Charles M. Atkinson, general editor

RECENT RESEARCHES IN THE MUSIC OF THE RENAISSANCE
    James Haar, general editor

RECENT RESEARCHES IN THE MUSIC OF THE BAROQUE ERA
    Steven Saunders, general editor

RECENT RESEARCHES IN THE MUSIC OF THE CLASSICAL ERA
    Neal Zaslaw, general editor

RECENT RESEARCHES IN THE MUSIC OF THE NINETEENTH AND EARLY TWENTIETH CENTURIES
    Rufus Hallmark, general editor

RECENT RESEARCHES IN AMERICAN MUSIC
    John M. Graziano, general editor

RECENT RESEARCHES IN THE ORAL TRADITIONS OF MUSIC
    Philip V. Bohlman, general editor

Each edition in *Recent Researches* is devoted to works by a single composer or to a single genre. The content is chosen for its high quality and historical importance and is edited according to the scholarly standards that govern the making of all reliable editions.

For information on establishing a standing order to any of our series, or for editorial guidelines on submitting proposals, please contact:

A-R Editions, Inc.
Middleton, Wisconsin

800 736-0070 (North American book orders)
608 836-9000 (phone)
608 831-8200 (fax)
http://www.areditions.com

RECENT RESEARCHES IN THE MUSIC OF THE BAROQUE ERA, 181

# Alessandro Scarlatti

# Selected Sacred Music

Edited by Luca Della Libera

**A-R Editions, Inc.**
Middleton, Wisconsin

To my wife, Teresa

A-R Editions, Inc., Middleton, Wisconsin
© 2012 by A-R Editions, Inc.

All rights reserved. No part of this book may be reproduced
or transmitted in any form by any electronic or mechanical
means (including photocopying, recording, or information
storage and retrieval) without permission in writing from
the publisher.

The purchase of this edition does not convey the right to
perform it in public, nor to make a recording of it for any
purpose. Such permission must be obtained in advance
from the publisher.

A-R Editions is pleased to support scholars and performers
in their use of *Recent Researches* material for study or performance.
Please visit our website (www.areditions.com) to
apply for permission to perform, record, or otherwise reuse
the material in this publication.

Alessandro Scarlatti, *Miserere* is from Capp. Sist. 188–89,
© 2012 Biblioteca Apostolica Vaticana, and may not be
republished or performed without the written permission of
the Biblioteca Apostolica Vaticana.

Printed in the United States of America

ISBN 978-0-89579-742-1
ISSN 0484-0828

♾ The paper used in this publication meets the minimum
requirements of the American National Standard for
Information Sciences—Permanence of Paper for Printed
Library Materials, ANSI Z39.48-1992.

# Contents

Acknowledgments   vi

Introduction   vii

   Scarlatti in Rome, 1703–8   vii
   The Return to Naples and the *Missa defunctorum*   ix
   The Music of the Edition   ix
   Notes on Performance   xiii
   Notes   xiv

Plates   xvii

*Salve Regina*   1

*Miserere*   11

*Magnificat*   22

*Missa defunctorum*   63

   Introit: "Requiem aeternam dona eis Domine"   63
   Kyrie   68
   Gradual: "Requiem aeternam—Absolve, Domine"   71
   Sequence: "Dies irae, dies illa"   77
   Offertory: "Domine Jesu Christe"   91
   Sanctus   99
   Agnus Dei   103
   Communion: "Lux aeterna"   108

Critical Report   113

   Sources   113
   Editorial Methods   114
   Critical Notes   115
   Notes   116

# Acknowledgments

This edition would not have been possible without the assistance of many musicians and colleagues. Thanks to musicians who volunteered to perform these compositions, I had the valuable opportunity to hear them and to check some aspects of my transcriptions that otherwise might not have been observed. Thus I wish to thank Rinaldo Alessandrini, Konrad Junghänel, and Pascal Duc. For the preparation of the commentaries I received useful, precious suggestions from Warren Kirkendale. I also wish to thank Dinko Fabris and Romano Vettori; Marcello Eynard and Maurizio Capuano of the library "Angelo Mai" in Bergamo; and the staffs of the Fitzwilliam Museum in Cambridge, the Münster Diözesanbibliothek, and the Biblioteca Apostolica Vaticana.

# Introduction

Alessandro Scarlatti's sacred music might, at first glance, be divisible into two basic groupings: those works in the *concertato* medium, including obbligato instruments and modern, operatic musical devices; and those in a more conservative vein, scored only for voices or voices and continuo.[1] This last category, however, cannot be simply designated with the conventional terms "a cappella" or "stile antico"; this is due partly to the stylistic mileu of Rome at the turn of the eighteenth century, but more to Scarlatti's own stylistic flexibility. His works, in fact, may have stretched even the bounds of contemporary theoretical terminology: according to the composer and music theorist Girolamo Chiti (1679–1759), Giuseppe Ottavio Pitoni (who was Chiti's teacher in the field of the sacred music) had classified the style of Scarlatti (together with that of Gesualdo da Venosa) as "Stile imperfetto detto tolerabile" (imperfect but tolerated).[2] Of the pieces in the present volume, the *Miserere* and the *Salve Regina* might be placed, according to common assumption, in the *di cappella* style,[3] but the same cannot be said of the *Magnificat* and the *Missa defunctorum,* which each in their own way augment that basic texture with more heterogenous styles. This last piece has been labeled as *stile antico*,[4] but a close look at contemporary terminology in Italy does not support this usage. A better classification might be "stile pieno," or "sollevato"; that is, characterized by the presence of the *basso seguente*, by the alternation of passages of homophony and of free counterpoint, as well as chromatic alterations and dissonances. The *Magnificat* presents in addition to these elements some soloistic sections in the *stile concertato* amid a wide variety of notation.[5] I have chosen these four compositions because, in spite of the different scorings, stylistic features, and biographical periods they represent, they have an important element in common: the presence of stylistic traits that, on the one hand, are derived from those of Palestrina, and, on the other, show a particular attention to advanced expressive techniques, as I have also observed in two recent articles.[6] The critical edition of these selected compositions may help to enrich the acquaintance of this repertoire still too little explored by scholars and musicians, amend the lack of modern editions, and focus more precisely on the characteristics of the sacred music of the great Sicilian composer.

## Scarlatti in Rome, 1703–8

The historical context for those pieces presented here that can be dated begins with Scarlatti's employment in Rome. Although we don't know the circumstances surrounding the composition of the *Magnificat,* it may stem from Scarlatti's prior job as director of the Real Cappella in Naples, a position he held from 1684 to 1702.[7] His last years in Naples were marked by financial insecurity and numerous efforts to obtain employment and commissions elsewhere, especially Rome and Florence. The situation became even more precarious after the death of King Charles II of Spain on 1 November 1700, during the War of the Spanish Succession, in which the Bourbons contended with the Hapsburgs for the Spanish crown and its possessions, including Naples.[8] Conspiracies and murders were rampant, and it became clear to Scarlatti that Naples, which had received him so generously eighteen years earlier, no longer guaranteed him and his large family a secure professional future. He obtained a leave of absence and brought his family on an ill-fated trip to Florence, where he hoped find a stable position with Ferdinando de' Medici.[9]

Stopping in Rome during his return from Florence to Naples, Scarlatti thought to find accommodation, evidently makeshift, in the "eternal city" for himself and his family. In a letter of 16 January 1703 to the Florentine impresario Luca Casimiro degli Albizzi, the granducal agent in Naples, Giovanni Battista Salomoni, wrote:

> Sig. Alessandro Scarlatti, with the greater part of his family, particularly all the females, came to Rome Saturday morning. His intention was indeed to detach himself from [Naples] and with this in mind he had resigned from the royal chapel. But the lord viceroy [Luis Francisco de la Cerda y Aragon, duke of Medinaceli (1660–1711)], either for pity or to evade the grave misfortunes of this chapel, did not give him leave for more than two months. In any case, if he should find an adequate niche in Rome, he will arrange to stay there, but he will never be able to succeed with the advantage that he had in this city.[10]

Scarlatti's concerns about his own future must have been very strong to induce him to return to a city that, twenty years earlier, he had left precisely because of the unfavorable conditions for opera. The intervening time had not improved the situation. In Rome, under the pontificate of Innocent XII (1691–1700), public performances of operas had been rigorously prohibited, and thus many theaters, including the Capranica, were closed, and the Tordinona was demolished in 1697. A series of circumstances also curtailed theatrical life in Rome in the first decade of the eighteenth century: the Holy Year 1700, the extraordinary Holy Year of 1702 motivated by the war, the earthquakes of 1703, and the subsequent prohibition by the pontifical authorities of every public entertainment for five years. In fact, Scarlatti found the circumstances in Rome in 1703 to be quite the same as before: operatic productions were replaced by oratorios, which found their most important venue in the church of Santa Maria in Vallicella (better known as the Chiesa Nuova).

However, in Rome Scarlatti could enjoy the esteem and protection of Cardinal Pietro Ottoboni, who had been the librettist for Scarlatti's *La Statira* (1690), *La Giuditta* "di Napoli" (1694), and *L'Oratorio per la Santissima Annunziata* (1700). In April 1702 Ottoboni had some of Scarlatti's Lamentations settings performed in the Palazzo della Cancelleria during an *accademia* in which music of Corelli was also performed.[11] Ottoboni was also protector of the Congregation of the Oratorio in the Chiesa Nuova, and evidently Scarlatti owed to him and to Cardinal Galeazzo Marescotti the appointment he received on 9 January 1703 as *coadiutore* to Giovanni Bicilli. Scarlatti was hired, albeit after some discussion, without a salary, but with the guarantee to succeed Bicilli.[12]

The manuscript of the *Salve Regina* in this edition is one of the few Scarlatti autographs of sacred music with a date, namely February 1703, one month after his appointment at the Chiesa Nuova. It was probably performed during the service of the *Quaranta ore* during Lent in 1703 in the Roman basilica of San Lorenzo in Damaso, which was annexed to Cardinal Ottoboni's Palazzo della Cancelleria. Violent earthquakes on 14 January and 2 February had caused damage that prevented the use of the Chiesa Nuova, and Cardinal Ottoboni organized a function "with magnificent pomp" (*con magnifica pompa*) on 17 March at San Lorenzo in Damaso, exhibiting the *Santissimo Sacramento* in thanksgiving to God and the Virgin Mary for having protected Rome from the earthquake.[13] Although polychoral music was more frequently performed at Ottoboni's services, there is archival documentation that works for four voices were performed as well.[14]

The *Miserere* presented in this edition, which is preserved in the Cappella Sistina collection at the Vatican Library, also stems from Scarlatti's stay in Rome. Although Roberto Pagano and others have dated it from 1680,[15] it was more likely performed at the Sistine Chapel for the first and probably the only time in 1708.[16] Pagano took his information from Giuseppe Baini:

> To increase, however, the beauty of Allegri's *Miserere*, the annoyance increased when hearing others, which could not compare with it. From Alessandro Scarlatti, a famous name from the school of Naples and worthy teacher of his son Domenico and of Adolf Hasse, called the Saxon, the college obtained about 1680 a new *Miserere*, but the work did not correspond to the fame of the composer, and this *Miserere* adopted by the chapel out of respect and expediency, alternated on Maundy Thursday, in place of that by Naldini, with the *Miserere* of Felice Anerio. . . . From 1714 until 1767 inclusively the two *Miserere* of Allegri and Bai shared the applause of the listeners in the three matins of Tenebrae, and the *Miserere* of Felice Anerio and Scarlatti were never again sung in our chapel.[17]

Baini's remark about "the fame of the composer," written over a hundred years after the fact, obscures a problem with the 1680 date for Scarlatti's *Miserere*: it is very unlikely that the college of the Sistine Chapel would commission such an important work for their own repertoire of the Easter liturgy from a twenty-year-old composer at the beginning of his career, with little experience in the area of sacred music and not yet introduced to the papal court. The only testimony describing a performance of the *Miserere* dates from Maundy Thursday, 1708. In the *Diario Sistino* of that year one reads:

> In the *Miserere* of Sig. Scarlatti the voice in a verse was taken a tone lower by the plainchant choir, for which the following gentlemen were [each] fined 20 baiocchi: Perrini, Sauli, Petrucci, Iacobelli, Mattia, Bastianelli, Ma[e]stro, Anatò, Cinotti, Viviani, Mossi, Rossi, Monaci, Paolo Besci, Tiepoli, Pippi, Nicolai.
>
> And because in the second polyphonic chorus the tenor and altus, entering together, the latter before the tenor in the lowered tone of the choir, and the tenor did not enter until the bass was heard to enter, also the *puntatore* was fined 20 baiocchi.
>
> The others who sang in the polyphonic choir are not fined, not even Sig. Carli, who by a resolution of the college is excluded from the fines.[18]

A search through the *Diari Sistini* of the last two decades of the seventeenth century and the first decade of the eighteenth did not reveal information on any other performances.[19] It is mentioned by Andrea Adami in 1711 among the pieces available for Maundy Thursday:

> The *Miserere* is by Sig. Scarlatti for two choirs, the other one is by Felice Anerio for two choirs, book 88, folio 28, whence the master can select one at his pleasure.[20]

But the *Diario Sistino* informs us that Allegri's *Miserere* was performed on that day:

> On Maundy Thursday was sung the first Lamentation of Gregorio Allegri in four-part polyphony and the *Miserere* for two choirs by the same author. This day there appeared with our choir His Serene Highness, the Prince Alexander, son of King John of Poland, with the dispensation of His Holiness, with two others in his company, and the famous performance of the said *Miserere* was much applauded.[21]

This source also testifies that, three years after the first performance, Scarlatti's *Miserere* was not available in the archive: the manuscript preserved in the Vatican Library was copied by Tommaso Altavilla in 1711, evidently after Adami's mention. It may be that 1708 was the only performance of the *Miserere* during Scarlatti's lifetime.

Lent 1708 was a particularly productive period for the composer. On 25 March, the Feast of the Annunciation, his *Oratorio per la Santissima Annuziata* was performed in the Palazzo della Cancelleria, very probably a revival of the 1703 performance in the Chiesa Nuova. On 26 February his oratorio *Il giardino di rose* was presented by Francesco Maria Ruspoli in the Palazzo Bonelli (after being heard on 3 and 24 April 1707 in Massa and Rome, respectively).[22] And on 4 April, Ash Wednesday, again in the Cancelleria, the *Oratorio per la Passione di Nostro Signore Gesù Cristo* was repeated (probably for the third year in succession), a few days before the celebrated first performance of Handel's *La Resurrezione,* on 8 April, Easter Sunday. The three oratorios on the Annunciation, Passion, and Resurrection of Christ in "chronological-biographical" sequence were surely conceived as a cycle.[23]

The exclusion of Scarlatti's *Miserere* from the repertoire of the Sistine Chapel raises the issue of musical aesthetics in the chapel. Baini's above-quoted criticisms suggest a certain intolerance toward novelty, also betrayed by his appreciation of the *Miserere* of Tommaso Bai:

> At the request of the college, Tommaso Bai, from Crevalcuore near Bologna, chapel master of the Vatican basilica, wrote in 1714 a new *Miserere* with one verse for five, another for four, and the last for eight voices, on the melodies of the *Miserere* of Allegri, and also having varied other verses a little, but with very bright and simple and at the same time sublime melodies, he obtained the greatest applause, and perpetuated his glory with this single production.[24]

Baini's date is incorrect: Bai composed his *Miserere* in 1711. The source is the *Diario Sistino* of that year:

> [Maundy Thursday] was sung the *Miserere* of Signor Thomaso Baij, singer of the Vatican basilica, after it was presented to His Holiness, who was pleased to accept it, and sent it to the cardinal protector so that, having been recognized for the purpose, it would be sung, which resulted in general applause.[25]

The decision to exclude Scarlatti's *Miserere* was probably based on the fact that it was too far from Allegri's model, which is primarily notable for the ease with which it can be ornamented by the singers.[26]

Although Scarlatti's activities in Rome were intense, they failed to provide the increase in income he had hoped for, and on 1 December he was recalled to his old position as master of the Real Cappella in Naples by the viceroy, Cardinal Grimani.

## The Return to Naples and the *Missa defunctorum*

In this period Scarlatti resumed his activity as a composer of operas, sacred music, and instrumental music. It is not known for what occasion Scarlatti composed the *Missa defunctorum*, and we can now present only some hypotheses. The manuscript is dated 1717, a year for which we have scarce information on the composer's activity. We know that at the end of March the oratorio *La vergine addolorata* was performed in Naples and Salerno,[27] and that he composed the two intermezzi *Vespetta e Milo*, on Silvio Stampiglia's libretto, for the pastoral opera *Giove in Argo*, which was performed with music by Antonio Lotti in Dresden during the fall. The *Missa defunctorum* may have been composed on the occasion of the premature death of the heir to the imperial throne, Archduke Leopold, on 4 November 1716 at the age of only six months. He had been born eight years into the imperial couple's marriage, and it is evident how deeply this misfortune was also felt in Naples. The Real Cappella, directed in those years by Scarlatti, had among its duties to be present not only at solemn ceremonies of the viceregal court, but also at those celebrated in Naples for the imperial family. We know, for example, that when Emperor Joseph I died in 1711, the chapel participated in ceremonies for several days.[28] Scarlatti himself composed in 1716 the splendid serenata *La Gloria di primavera* to celebrate the long-awaited birth of Archduke Leopold. On the other hand, the lack of instruments (of which a good number were available in the royal chapel) in the *Missa defunctorum* suggests that it was composed and performed for a private occasion and context.

## The Music of the Edition

### Salve Regina

Scarlatti composed four settings of the *Salve Regina*:

*Salve Regina* [I], for SATB, February 1703 (included in the present volume).
*Salve Regina* [II], for SATB, 2 Vns., B.c., the composition that concludes the *Mottetti sacri,* published 1702 (possibly also in 1697) in Naples, and the *Concerti sacri,* published 1707–8 in Amsterdam.[29]
*Salve Regina* [III], for S, 2 Vns., Va., B.c., presumably composed before 1715.[30]
*Salve Regina* [IV], for S, 3 Vns., Va., B.c., presumably composed after 1715.[31]

The *Salve Regina* I is very different from the other three settings and is a particularly striking example of Scarlatti's adaption of the *stile di cappella*. First of all, the choice of the vocal ensemble CATB, as well as the contrapuntal writing, adheres to the stylistic framework of the *stile di cappella*.[32] None of the four voices assumes a predominant role. The absence of a harmonic support by a basso continuo further highlights the texture. Moreover, unlike the *Salve Regina* III and IV, but like the *Salve Regina* II, the work is not subdivided into separate sections, but consists of a single movement without any change of meter or scoring. The "severe" frame of this piece is enforced also by the use of the first four notes of the plainchant antiphon, like a tenor that circulates through the entire composition in the different voices. Scarlatti had already used this treatment effectively in the *Salve Regina* II, where the plainchant melody is distributed not only among the voices, but also among the two *concertanti* violins. In the *Salve Regina* I the first four measures, in which all voices intone the word "Salve," are constructed as a true *lamento*: the four melodic lines are based on the descending tetrachord, though with different rhythmic figures. The first phrase concludes with a cadence on the fifth degree, enriched by a 4–3 suspension in the altus (m. 4), while the different rhythmic profiles of the voices create expressive suspensions. At measures 5–7 the word "Salve" is repeated and the bassus intones the plainchant melody. A stylistic feature also found in the *Miserere* is the chromatic inflection of certain melodic formulations, as in the altus and tenor for "Vita dulcedo," measures 11–14. The plainchant melody returns as a kind of "frame" in the appearance of the word "Salve," the *salutation*, which is repeated with this melody twice in the bassus (mm. 17–18 and 21–23), once in the altus (mm. 19–20), and once in the tenor (mm. 18–20). In the bassus it is set a tone higher the second time (mm. 21–23) as the rhetorical figure of *climax*.

The second section, "Ad te clamamus," is lively and brief, followed by a more meditative moment on the words "exsules, filii Evae." These are preceded by a rest in all voices and set in a middle-low range, in accord with the sense of the text. There follows a sudden change of mode (from major to minor) on the word "filii" (m. 34). This section has some features in common with the *Salve Regina* II: the general rest after the word "clamamus" and the same sudden change of mode, in that instance on the word "exsules." We find this effect also near the end of the *Salve Regina* I (m. 117) on the repetition of the word "dulcis," intoned with the interval of an ascending minor third in the altus. For "Ad te suspiramus" Scarlatti uses the same incipit as "Ad te clamamus" but in contrary motion, beginning with an imitative three-part texture (CAT) that stresses the syllables "su-" and "-spi-," which is repeated in the altus and bassus with a chromatic extension (m. 41). Similar chromatic inflections with expressive functions are present for "gementes et flentes" (mm. 42–47). With the phrase "in hac lacrimarum valle" the four voices draw a descending melodic line, very articulated and richly dissonant, with a marked rhetorical device for the word "lacrimarum," which is sung by the cantus and tenor to an augmented fourth (mm. 49 and 51). Scarlatti then adds a repetition of the salutation "Salve" to emphasize the concluding tonality of the section (F major), using again the melody of the plainchant antiphon in the bassus (mm. 59–61). We find the same situation after "ad nos converte," where once again the salutation "Salve" is added and repeated several times, with the plainchant melody first in the cantus, then in the bassus (mm. 79–84). Later we find in the bassus an extended line of long notes (semibreves) with chromatic inflection for "O dulcis virgo Maria," repeated three times (mm. 111–25).

## Miserere

Scarlatti composed four *Miserere* settings:

> *Miserere* [I], for choir SATB, choir SSATB, 1708 (included in the present volume).
> *Miserere* [II], for solo SSATB, choir SATB, 2 Vns., Va., B.c., 1714?
> *Miserere* [III], for solo SSATB, choir SATB, 2 Vns., Va., B.c., 1715?
> *Miserere* [IV], for SATB, B.c., 1721?[33]

In *Miserere* I, Scarlatti partly follows the model of Allegri's *Miserere*, whose contemporary fame is testified to by Andrea Adami:

> Among these worthy composers who deserve eternal praise equal to all the others is our companion Gregorio Allegri, who with few, but so well chosen and more judicious notes composed the *Miserere* that is sung on that day [Maundy Wednesday] every year, rendered a true miracle of our time, for having been conceived with such proportions as to ravish the soul of the listener.[34]

The vocal ensemble is the same in both works: two choirs (CATB and CCATB), which are combined only in the final section, "tunc imponent."[35] Allegri's model is present also in the choice to leave the even-numbered verses to plainchant, in the choice of the key, and in the cyclic form of the psalm. But Scarlatti's score, which was composed around sixty years later than Allegri's, is much more refined and complex:[36] each choir is assigned a different formal model; the initial and final sections are free; and the alternation between falsobordone and free sections is much more varied than in Allegri's setting.[37] Above all, we see the difference between Allegri's strophic form and Scarlatti's more articulated design (see table 1).[38] As is evident, there is in Scarlatti's more complex structure a certain symmetry in the distribution of the musical substance. Not only is the overall form much more articulated than that of Allegri, but there is also more varied articulation within each psalm verse in both the formal and harmonic aspect. The setting of the fifth verse, "Tibi soli peccavi," provides an example. In Allegri's version the text is set simply in two sections, each beginning with falsobordone and ending with a cadential figure, the verse being divided as it would in chant.[39] In Scarlatti's setting, by contrast, the falsobordone and cadential sections are set off by sections of free polyphony. The initial falsobordone on "Tibi soli" is immediately followed by an intermediate cadential figure in measures 32–34, a free section in measure 34, and another cadence in measures 35–36. In the second half of the verse, the falsobordone setting of "ut justificeris" (mm. 37–38) is likewise followed by a section of free polyphony (mm. 39–40), a cadence in measure 40, and another free section (mm. 41–45) before the cadence at the end of the verse.

The richness and variety of Scarlatti's harmonic language are also far removed from the model of Allegri, especially in some moments of particular harshness, such as the expressive dissonance on the words "iniquitate" (mm. 19–20) and "peccavi" (m. 33). In the first case, the syncopated rhythm in the first cantus amplifies the effect of the dissonance. In the second case, the bassus and cantus proceed by thirds in a rising semitone, an interval often used to express intense pathos. At the same time the bassus clashes with the altus (a♭/g′) and with the d′ held in the tenor. The cadential formulas used to conclude the various verses provide examples of chromatic inflection in addition to the usual long notes with expressive suspensions (mm. 45–46 and 128–29).

## Magnificat

Scarlatti composed three *Magnificat* settings:

> *Magnificat* [I], for solo SSATB, choir SSATB, 2 Vns., Va., Vc., B.c., within a vespers cycle composed between 1720 and 1721 for the basilica of Santa Cecilia in Trastevere in Rome.
> *Magnificat* [II], for solo SSAT, choir SSATB, B.c., before 1715 (included in the present volume).

TABLE 1
The *Miserere*: Formal Structure in Allegri and Scarlatti

| Verse | | Gregorio Allegri | | Alessandro Scarlatti | |
|---|---|---|---|---|---|
| 1   | Miserere mei, Deus    | I    | A | I    | A |
| 3   | Amplius lava me       | II   | B | II   | B |
| 5   | Tibi soli peccavi     | I    | A | I    | C |
| 7   | Ecce enim veritatem   | II   | B | II   | D |
| 9   | Auditui meo dabis     | I    | A | I    | E |
| 11  | Cor mundum            | II   | B | II   | B |
| 13  | Redde mihi laetitiam  | I    | A | I    | E |
| 15  | Libera me             | II   | B | II   | D |
| 17  | Quoniam si voluisses  | I    | A | I    | C |
| 19  | Benigne fac, Domine   | II   | B | II   | B |
| 20a | Tunc acceptabis       | I    | C |      |   |
| 20b | Tunc imponent         | I, II | C | I, II | F |

*Key.* I = primus chorus, II = secundus chorus, A–F = musical material

*Magnificat* [III], for solo SSATB, choir SSATB, 2 Vns., Va., B.c., presumably composed before 1715.[40]

The *Magnificat* II displays a unique synthesis of the Palestrinian model and the expressive language of the eighteenth century. Unlike the *Salve Regina* and the *Missa defunctorum*, the *Magnificat* is subdivided into various sections according to scoring, texture, and tonality (see table 2). The basso continuo is not always limited to doubling the vocal parts, but is sometimes autonomous, as at "Quia respexit" (mm. 52–66) and "Quia fecit" (mm. 76–98). Scarlatti's setting exploits the great richness and variety of the Marian text, especially the words tied to the emotional and descriptive spheres: (a) the verb "exaltare," in various forms; (b) the pulsating, dancing rhythm for "Et exsultavit spiritus meus"; (c) the ascending arpeggios on "Et exaltavit"; (d) the interval of a rising fourth and long repeated melismas for the adjective "potens"; (e) the descending lines for "deposuit" and "humiles"; (f) a dissonant interval (a rising diminished fourth) for "misericordiae suae"; and (g) the long virtuosi passages for "Gloria."

Jeanne Shaffer has identified the sections for which Scarlatti used melodic material derived from plainchant: "Magnificat," "Deposuit," "Esurientes," and "Sicut erat" (see table 2).[41] But she confused the plainchant sources: the first example she cites is taken not from the canticle, but from an alleluia verse.[42]

As in the *Miserere*, Scarlatti creates a more complex formal design than might be accounted for simply by referencing *stile di cappella* elements such as the use of chant and pervasive imitation. In fact, his design does depend on these elements, but also displays an eighteenth-century sensitivity to harmonic design and text expression. Scarlatti begins his *Magnificat* in an intimate atmosphere with only two voices (second cantus and altus), which makes room for the evocation of the plainchant melody in the second cantus, surrounded by delicate interlacing and momentary dissonances; for example, the major seventh chord that returns systematically on the tonic accent of the word "Magnificat." Expressive tension is also achieved by suggesting and evading cadential motion. For instance, in measures 4, 7, and 18 the cadential figures lead to 7–6 suspensions. In measure 10 the leading tone is withheld, as it is in measure 13, prolonging the harmonic outline of the phrase. Likewise, measure 15 is an imperfect authentic cadence (or a half cadence) in which a first-inversion seventh chord resolves downward by step to a root position triad (repeated in m. 17).

In the third and fourth sections, modern soloistic writing, complete with independent continuo parts, brings the piece suddenly into the *stile concertato*. Scarlatti's facility with dramatic vocal music can be seen in the brief chordal interludes on "omnes generationes" (mm. 67–75), and the lenghty virtuoso melismas on "potens" (mm. 77–88).

Scarlatti here is characteristically adept in his use of musico-rhetorical and text-expressive devices. "Et misericordia ejus" is characterized by dense chordal writing, beginning in the bass with the descending tetrachord, the topos of the *lamento*. "Fecit potentiam" has an imitative character, with significant figuration descending rapidly on the word "dispersit." The five-part writing returns in "Deposuit," with intervals specifically chosen for their affective impact, such as the rising fourth for "potentes" and the ascending arpeggios on "Et exaltavit." The following section, "Esurientes," assigned to the first and second cantus and tenor, is musically subdivided into two parts: the first up to "puerum tuum," the second with systematic use of the rising diminished fourth for "misericordiae suae" in the minor mode from the leading tone to the third degree, a figure repeated no less than eight times. The use of this interval to express lament is also found in the music of Luigi Rossi and Giovanni Battista Bassani; Pergolesi used it at the beginning of his *Stabat mater*, while Antonio Caldara had introduced it in inversion.[43] The phrase "Sicut locutus est" returns to

TABLE 2
Compositional Design of the *Magnificat*

| Measure | Text incipit | Tonality | Meter | Scoring | Texture |
|---|---|---|---|---|---|
| 1 | Magnificat | d–D | ¢ | CCATB | imitative with plainchant present |
| 26 | Et exsultavit | d–D | 3/2 | CCATB | imitative—chordal |
| 52 | Quia respexit | d–D | ¢ | C solo | soloistic |
| 67 | Omnes generationes | B♭–D | ¢ | CCATB | chordal |
| 76 | Quia fecit | d–D | ¢ | C solo | soloistic |
| 99 | Et misericordia | d–A | 3/2 | CCATB | chordal |
| 116 | Fecit potentiam | F–F | ¢ | CAT | imitative |
| 146 | Deposuit potentes | d–D | ¢* | CCATB | imitative with plainchant present |
| 184 | Esurientes | d–D | ¢ | CCT | imitative with plainchant present |
| 258 | Sicut locutus | g–D | 3/2 | CCATB | chordal |
| 276 | Gloria Patri | d–a | ¢ | CC solo | soloistic |
| 284 | Et Filio | a–D | ¢ | CCATB | chordal |
| 292 | Sicut erat | d–D | ¢ | CCATB | imitative with plainchant present |
| 347 | Et in saecula | d–D | 3/2 | CCATB | chordal |
| 358 | Amen | d–D | ¢ | CCATB | imitative |

* In the edition this section has been transcribed in ¢ to reflect the "Largo" tempo designation.

weighty homophonic writing, while "Gloria Patri" begins with virtuoso passages in the two cantus before the rapid choral conclusion. The "Sicut erat" is based on a contrapuntal construction in which the plainchant melody is set against a countersubject on "et nunc et semper," flowing directly into "et in saecula saeculorum" with a change of meter (3/2) and homorhythmic writing, before returning to counterpoint for the concluding "Amen." These striking and accomplished transitions between textures and styles can be explained neither as an imitation of Palestrina nor as a contemporary take on sacred music. Like the other pieces in this volume, the *Magnificat* points to a complex interaction between the idea of the *stile di cappella* and the expressive devices of contemporary dramatic music. In this particular piece, the intensity of contrast allows us an explicit glimpse into those interactions.

## *Missa defunctorum*

The *Missa defunctorum* exists in multiple manuscript sources (see the critical report below). All of the nineteenth-century manuscripts, however, stem from a copy that lacks the *Dies irae*, while the primary source, an partially autograph manuscript in Bergamo, is complete. Edward Dent judged Scarlatti's *Missa defunctorum* as "rather unequal," but he evidently did not know the autograph manuscript in Bergamo, since he maintained that it lacks the *Dies irae*.[44]

Between the second half of the seventeenth century and the first decades of the eighteenth there are not many Neapolitan settings of the Requiem. The source closest to Scarlatti is the *Missa defunctorum* of Francesco Provenzale preserved in some Neapolitan manuscripts.[45] Provenzale's original version was probably for four voices, but during the author's life it was performed with a more ample ensemble and the addition of a second choir. Dinko Fabris has hypothesized that the *Missa defunctorum* of Provenzale was performed on solemn occasions because it is written for two choirs and also contains the responsory "Libera me."[46] Among other settings are a *Missa defunctorum* for four voices and organ by Giovanni Salvatore, dated 1685, and one for two choirs by Cristoforo Caresana. Fabris notes that the first Neapolitan Requiem after that of Caresana is that in C minor by his pupil Nicola Fago, again for two choirs (each for five voices), with two trumpets, strings, and basso continuo.[47]

Scarlatti's *Missa defunctorum* is extremely compact and unified, as we see from the choice of a single tonality (D minor, the same as Provenzale) and the consistent employment of the four voices, excepting only the *Benedictus,* one verse from the Introit, and three from the Sequence.

The echoes of the Palestrinian tradition are very audible in the prevalently horizontal dimension of the writing and in the use of plainchant melody. Scarlatti quotes the plainchant in the cantus in measures 1–4 of the Introit, in the Agnus Dei on the words "Agnus Dei," and in the Communion on the words "quia pius est."[48]

The great compactness of the score is also due to techniques derived from the Renaissance cyclic mass, as in the identical first two measures of the Introit and Offertory. Ute Schacht-Pape noted four other passages similar to each other: measures 1–2 of the Kyrie, the verse "In memoria aeterna" of the Gradual, and the beginnings of the Sanctus and Agnus Dei. In the latter the similarity actually involves only the melody of the bass. Schacht-Pape also noted the use of the same rhythmic model in the first two measures of the Gradual, the Sequence, the Lacrimosa, and the Offertory (also at the beginning of the verse "Hostias et preces").[49] Another such similarity is found between the first measures of the Introit and the Gradual. Scarlatti also made extensive use of this device in his concerted masses, especially the *Messa per il Santissimo Natale* and in the *Messa breve e concertata*, which he composed as chapel master at Santa Maria Maggiore in Rome.[50] Besides these choices, rooted in the Renaissance, Scarlatti adopted another, tied to the baroque era, to underline the work's cohesion: the descending tetrachord—the topos of the *lamento,* which we have observed already in the *Salve Regina* and *Magnificat.* It is used several times during the course of the score, almost always for the invocation "dona eis," which in this way acquires notable and conspicuous expressive power. We find the tetrachord in the Introit, where, in the double initial imploration "dona eis, Domine" (mm. 5–12) it is repeated twice contrapuntally in all voices. The same treatment is found, further on, in a similar imploration, "dona eis requiem," repeated several times at the end of the Sequence (mm. 167–79). In the final section the tetrachord fulfills the function of a "frame" with the invocation "dona eis pacem" in the Communion. In this case it is present in the tenor, in its simplest version, for "dona eis" (mm. 48–49), while in the bassus and basso continuo its role is emphasized by means of more dilated writing, enriched with chromatic passages on "dona eis, Domine" (mm. 48–52). A very close tie between the text and its music is in the "Lacrimosa" section of the Sequence, since Scarlatti signifies this specific word with a modified descending tetrachord, first in the tenor and bassus (mm. 144–45) and then, in the repetition, in a long melismatic melody in the altus (mm. 146–51). We have seen that Scarlatti also used this *topos* very conspicuously in the *Salve Regina,* as he did again in the motet *Beata mater* that is preserved in an autograph in the archive of Santa Maria Maggiore in Rome.[51]

Another element that contributes to the coherence of the *Missa defunctorum* is the repetition of rhythmic-melodic modules, especially where the Latin text is not particularly long and Scarlatti opted to repeat entire verses, or parts of them, according to rhetorical criteria. This happens, for example, in the Introit. In the Sequence, on the other hand, which presents a long series of rhymed strophes grouped in threes, he reserves this repetitive articulation for cadences at the end of each strophe, otherwise avoiding this expedient (with the significant exception of the "Lacrimosa").

Unlike the *Requiem* of Provenzale and those of some non-Neapolitan composers (for example Francesco Cavalli and Giuseppe Ottavio Pitoni) who preferred a chordal texture, contrapuntal writing prevails in Scarlatti's *Missa defunctorum.* Only a few passages are homophonic: the triple meter setting of "Pleni sunt caeli" in the Sanctus (mm. 21–26), and the beginning of the Benedictus (m. 46). Echoes of the madrigal tradition are present in some descriptive passages, such as the verse "et de profundo lacu" in the Offertory (mm. 26–29), with a descent in imitation between the voices, consisting of downward leaps of an octave or fifth, culminating in the F♯ in the bassus, the lowest note in the entire score. Scarlatti uses similar devices in his motet *De profundo lacu,* in the instrumental introduction of the first aria (*De profundo lacu*) and also in the last one, *De profundis nos clamamus.*[52] Cavalli, in the corresponding passage of his *Requiem a otto voci,* has the bass descend still lower (to E), but the writing is homophonic and less madrigalesque compared to Scarlatti. Shortly afterward in Scarlatti's Offertory, on the verse "ne cadant in obscurum," we find a similar setting with descending melismas in quarter notes and imitation on the word "cadant" (mm. 39–42).

Notwithstanding the severe frame, Scarlatti chooses for some passages a very rich harmony: for example, measures 1–12 of the Introit, where the cadence arrives only after a long series of suspensions pregnant with seventh and ninth chords. Suspensions are also used significantly for an expressive function in the "Lacrimosa," precisely on the syllable "-cri-" (mm. 144 and 146 of the Sequence), to underline the harshness of this word. Similar examples are the ninth chord for the adjective "aeternam" in the Introit (m. 2) and for "stricte" and "cuncta" in the verse "Cuncta stricte discussurus" of the Sequence (mm. 16–21), which also reinforces the harsh sound of those words. In addition there are moments of great expressive weight, such as the first measure of the "Lacrimosa," rich in chromatic oscillations that recall Gesualdo, and the long melismas on dissonant harmonies in all voices on the last syllable of "lacrimosa" (mm. 147–50).

## Notes on Performance

One of the most relevant questions raised by this repertoire is that of performance forces. Fortunately, we know precisely the number of musicians for what was very probably the first performance of the *Miserere* on 5 April 1708, in the Sistine Chapel. The document quoted above informs us of the exact number of singers, both for the verses in plainchant and for the two choirs for those set polyphonically. From the *Diario Sistino* of 1708 we know also that the chapel consisted of thirty-eight singers (eleven "giubilati" and twenty-seven "serventi"): among them there were four "ufficiali" (the maestro di cappella, *decano, camerlengo,* and *puntatore*).[53] The document refers to the "puntature" (fines) imposed on the seventeen singers of the plainchant verses. The same diary informs us that on that day all the singers (both "serventi" and the "giubilati") were present at the service, with two exceptions: Andrea Adami and Girolamo Bigelli.[54] At the same time, we know that there was a long-standing tradition of performing the *Miserere* with one voice to a part, and this scoring was used for a performance of Allegri's *Miserere* during Holy Week of 1686.[55] According to Andrea Adami, the singers for the *Miserere* were chosen by the maestro di cappella,[56] and they were listed by the *puntatore* in some of the seventeenth-century *Diari Sistini.* Although there is no such list in the *Diario Sistino* of 1708 (quoted above in "Scarlatti in Rome, 1703–8"), the mention of "il tenore e il contralto" in the singular suggests that the scoring for Scarlatti's *Miserere* featured one singer per part as well.

Although it is difficult to specify the musical forces used for the *Magnificat* and the *Missa defunctorum,* we do know the number of musicians employed in the Neapolitan Real Cappella in the first decades of the eighteenth century. In June 1702 it was composed of five sopranos, two contraltos, five tenors, four basses, four

xiii

organists, two archlutenists, eight violinists, two violists, one harpist, and one doublebassist.[57] In December 1704 it was composed of five sopranos, four contraltos, seven tenors, four basses, three organists, twelve violinists, three cellists, one doublebassist, two archlutenists, one bassoonist, and two oboist/flutists.[58] In October 1708 there were three sopranos, five contraltos, four tenors, four basses, four organists, two archlutenists, two violists, one doublebassist, ten violinists, and one bassoonist; Scarlatti's return in December did not see substantial changes.[59]

Tempo indications are seldom found in the sources. Those that do occur, as with most of the time-words of the baroque era, often relate to mood, not to tempo.[60] For the *Miserere*, we have information from Adami regarding the performance of the last verse, which he describes as "smorzando poco à poco."[61] At the beginning of the *Missa defunctorum*, in the Introit, the note "à battuta giusta" suggests a regular, measured tempo.[62] In an autograph note on the Sequence we read "Si canta a battuta moderata, di due tempi, sì, ma non stretta" (a moderate beat, of two tempi, thus, but not rushed). The specificity of this indication shows the importance of a correct tempo for Scarlatti. In the "Lacrimosa" the indication "Adagio" can be interpreted by the singers, according to Brossard, as "at their ease, without pressing on, thus almost always slow and dragging the speed a little."[63] The last tempo marking, "Largo," occurs in the *Magnificat* at measure 52, the beginning of a section for solo cantus and basso continuo. The use of the term here seems consistent with its meaning in Brossard, where it is defined as conveying both a slow tempo and a certain flexibility of the beat.[64] A possible selection of tempi can be heard in the broadcast of three of the works in this anthology (*Missa defunctorum*, *Miserere*, and *Salve Regina*) on 14 November 2010 in Herne, performed by Cantus Colln under the direction of Konrad Junghänel, recorded by the radio WDR3, and now accessible via the Internet.[65] The *Magnificat* and the *Salve Regina* were recorded by Rinaldo Alessandrini with "Concerto italiano."[66]

It is difficult to say whether instruments were used in the *Magnificat* and *Missa defunctorum* to double the organ, because we do not know the precise context of their composition. This kind of "basso seguente" accompaniment, in which the basso continuo always doubles the lower voice, does not necessarily require a low string instrument.[67]

# Notes

1. Examples of Scarlatti's sacred music can be found in *Masses by Alessandro Scarlatti and Francesco Gasparini: Music from the Basilica of Santa Maria Maggiore, Rome*, ed. Luca Della Libera, Recent Researches in the Music of the Baroque Era, vol. 137 (Middleton, Wis.: A-R Editions, 2004); and Alessandro Scarlatti, *Concerti sacri, opera seconda*, ed. Luca Della Libera, Recent Researches in the Music of the Baroque Era, vol. 153 (Middleton, Wis.: A-R Editions, 2008).

2. The quotation is in a letter written by Chiti to Padre Martini, on 6 Semptember 1746; quoted in Anne Schnoebelen, *Padre Martini's Collection of Letters in the Civico Museo Bibliografico Musicale in Bologna: An Annotated Index* (New York: Pendragon Press, 1979), 148. The entire collection of the letters is now available free online: http://badigit.comune.bologna.it/cmbm/scripts/lettere/search.asp.

3. The term "Stil di Cappella" is used by Andrea Adami in Rome in 1711, writing on the music of Papal Chapel singer and composer Matteo Simonelli (after 1618–96), "Il Palestrina de' nostri tempi." See Andrea Adami da Bolsena, *Osservazioni per ben regolare il coro de i cantori della Cappella Pontificia* (Rome, 1711; facs. ed. by Giancarlo Rostirolla [Lucca: Libreria Italiana Editrice, 1988]), 209. See also Arnaldo Morelli, " 'Schola romana,' 'Stil di cappella' e cerimoniale papale," in *Musici e istituzioni musicali a Roma e nello Stato pontificio nel tardo Rinascimento: Attorno a Giovanni Maria Nanino, Atti della Giornata internazionale di studio, Tivoli, Villa d'Este, 26 ottobre 2007*, ed. Giorgio Monari and Federico Vizzaccaro (Tivoli: Società Tiburtina di Storia e d'Arte, 2008), 129–39; Federico Vizzaccaro, "Tipologie stilistico-compositive nella musica sacra a Roma tra XVII e XVIII secolo," in *Giuseppe Ottavio Pitoni e la musica del suo tempo: Atti del Convegno internazionale di studi, Rieti, 28–29 aprile 2008*, ed. Gaetano Stella, 239–81 (Rome: Istituto Italiano per la Storia della Musica, 2009), 242; and Sergio Durante, "La 'Guida armonica' di Giuseppe Ottavio Pitoni: un documento sugli stili musicali in uso a Roma al tempo di Corelli," in *Nuovissimi studi corelliani: Atti del terzo congresso internazionale, Fusignano, 4–7 settembre 1980*, ed. Sergio Durante and Pierluigi Petrobelli (Florence: Olschki, 1982), 285–326.

4. Albert Charles Roeckle, "Eighteenth-Century Neapolitan Settings of the Requiem Mass: Structure and Style" (Ph.D. diss., The University of Texas at Austin, 1978), 57 n. 114; Ute Schacht-Pape, *Das Messenschaffen von Alessandro Scarlatti* (Frankfurt am Main: Peter Lang, 1993), 105.

5. Vizzaccaro, "Tipologie stilistico-compositive," 244–47.

6. Luca Della Libera, "La musica sacra di Alessandro Scarlatti durante il periodo romano di Händel," in *Georg Friedrich Händel in Rom: Beiträge der internationalen Tagung am deutschen historischen Institut in Rom 17–20 Oktober 2007*, ed. Sabine Ehrmann-Herfort and Matthias Schnettger (Kassel: Bärenreiter, 2010), 155–84; Luca Della Libera, "Il 'concerto' tra Alessandro Scarlatti e Corelli: Due modelli a confronto," in *Arcangelo Corelli fra mito e realtà storica: Nuove prospettive d'indagine musicologica e interdisciplinare nel 350° anniversario della nascita: Atti del congresso internazionale di studi, Fusignano, 11–14 settembre 2003*, ed. Gregory Barnett, Antonella D'Ovidio, and Stefano La Via (Florence: Olschki, 2007), 2:507–22.

7. Benedikt Johannes Poensgen, "Die Offiziumskompositionen von Alessandro Scarlatti" (Ph.D. diss., University of Hamburg, 2004), 1:16.

8. Ursula Kirkendale, "The War of the Spanish Succession Reflected in Music by Antonio Caldara (Mantua, Milan, Vienna, Rome)," in *Music and Meaning: Studies in Music History and the Neighbouring Disciplines*, by Warren Kirkendale and Ursula Kirkendale (Florence: Olschki, 2007), 269–85.

9. On the relationship between Scarlatti and the prince, see Mario Fabbri, *Alessandro Scarlatti e il principe Ferdinando de' Medici* (Florence: Olschki, 1961); William C. Holmes, "Lettere inedite su Alessandro Scarlatti," in *La musica a Napoli durante il Seicento: Atti del convegno internazionale di studi: Napoli, 11–14 aprile 1985*, ed. Antonio Domenico D'Alessandro and Agostino Ziino (Rome: Torre d'Orfeo, 1987), 369–78.

10. "Il sig. Alessandro Scarlatti sabbato mattina, colla maggior parte della sua famiglia e particolarmente con tutte le sue femine, si portò a Roma. Il suo disegno era di staccarsi di qua affatto, al qual fine aveva rinuntiato la cappella reale; ma il sig. Vicerè, o per compassione di lui o per esimersi dalli gravi sorti per la detta cappella, non gli ha dato licenza che per due mesi. Ad ogni modo, s'egli troverà in Roma nicchia adeguata, farà in modo di fermarcesi, ma non potrà mai succedere col vantaggio che aveva in questa città." Holmes, "Lettere inedite," 376.

11. Poensgen, "Offiziumskompositionen," 1:24, n. 134. The Lamentations cited in the *Avvisi* quoted by Poensgen may have been a part of the well-known *Oratorio per la Passione di Nostro Signore*: Ottoboni, who wrote the libretto, also translated into Italian three Lamentations of Jeremiah.

12. Arnaldo Morelli, *"Il tempio armonico": Musica nell'Oratorio dei Filippini in Roma (1575–1705)* (Laaber: Laaber-Verlag, 1991), 137–38.

13. *Racconto istorico de terremoti sentiti in Roma . . . la sera de' 14 di Gennajo, e la mattina de' 2 di Febbrajo dell'anno 1703: Nel quale si narrano i danni fatti dal medesimo, le Sacre Missioni, il Giubbileo, le Processioni, e tutte le altre Divozioni, Funzioni, e Opere pie ordinate, e fatte dalla Santità di Nostro Signore Papa Clemente XI* (Rome: Chracas, 1704), 175.

14. Poensgen, "Offiziumskompositionen," 1:61.

15. Roberto Pagano, "Alessandro Scarlatti: Biografia," in *Alessandro Scarlatti*, by Roberto Pagano, Giancarlo Rostirolla, and Lino Bianchi (Turin: ERI, 1972), 51; Magda Marx-Weber, "Römische Vertonungen des Psalms Miserere im. 18. und frühen 19. Jahrhundert," *Hamburger Jahrbuch für Musikwissenschaft* 8 (1985): 12–13; Poensgen, "Offiziumskompositionen," 2:18.

16. On the *Miserere* tradition in the Sistine Chapel, see Magda Marx-Weber, "Die Tradition der Miserere-Vertonungen in der Cappella Pontificia," in *Collectanea II: Studien zur Geschichte der päpstlichen Kapelle: Tagungsbericht Heidelberg 1989*, ed. Bernhard Janz (Vatican City: Biblioteca Apostolica Vaticana, 1994), 266–88.

17. "Al crescere però le bellezze del *Miserere* dell'Allegri, cresceva la noja nell'udire gli altri, che non reggevano al paragone. Il collegio circa il 1680 ottenne da Alessandro Scarlatti, nome famoso della scuola di Napoli, e degno maestro di Domenico suo figlio, e di Adolfo Hasse, detto il Sassone, ottenne, dissi, un nuovo *Miserere*, ma l'opera non corrispose alla fama del compositore, e fu, questo *Miserere* dello Scarlatti adottato nella cappella, per rispetto e ripiego, ed alternato nel giovedì santo in luogo di quel del Naldini, con il *Miserere* di Felice Anerio. . . . Dal 1714 fino al 1767 inclusivamente li due *Miserere* dell'Allegri, e del Bai si divisero nei tre mattutini delle tenebre i plausi dell'uditorio, e mai più non si sono cantati nella nostra cappella i *Miserere* di Felice Anerio, e dello Scarlatti." Giuseppe Baini, *Memorie storico critiche della vita e delle opere di Giovanni Pierluigi da Palestrina* (Rome, 1828), 2:196–97 n. 578.

18. Biblioteca Apostolica Vaticana, Cappella Sistina, *Diario Sistino* 128 (1708), fols. 44r–45r.

"Nel Miserere del Sig. Scarlatti, dal choro del canto fermo fù pigliata in un verso la voce un tono più basso, perciò si puntano li ss.ri: [here follows a list in three columns]:

"[col. 1] Perrini b. 20   Sauli b. 20   Petrucci b. 20   Iacobelli b. 20   Mattia b. 20   Bastianelli b. 20 [col. 2] Ma[e]stro b. 20   Anatò [Hanoteau] b. 20   Cinotti b. 20   Viviani b. 20   Mossi b. 20 [col. 3] Rossi b. 20   Monaci b. 20   Paolo Besci b. 20   Tiepoli b. 20   Pippi b. 20   Nicolai b. 20

"E perché nel secondo choro del canto figurato entrando insieme il tenore, e contralto, questi attaccò prima del tenore in tono del choro calato et il tenore non entrò finchè non sentì entrato il Basso, si punta perciò anche il Puntatore.   B. 20.

"Gli altri che cantavano ne Chori del figurato non si puntano ne pure il Sig. Carli che per risolutione del Colleg.[i]o viene escluso da i punti e dalla spartizione di essi."

19. I was greatly helped in this search by information from Claudio Annibaldi.

20. "Il *Miserere* è di Alessandro Scarlatti a due Cori, l'altro è di Felice Anerio a due Cori lib. 88. a carte 28. onde il Signor Maestro potrà sceglierne uno a suo piacere." Adami, *Osservazioni per ben regolare il coro*, 41. On the repertory of the Sistine Chapel between the end of the sixteenth century and the beginning of the seventeenth century, see also Arnaldo Morelli, "Antimo Liberati, Matteo Simonelli e la tradizione palestriniana a Roma nella seconda metà del Seicento," in *Atti del II Convegno internazionale di studi palestriniani: Palestrina e la sua presenza nella musica e nella cultura europea dal suo tempo ad oggi, Palestrina, 3–5 maggio 1986*, ed. Lino Bianchi and Giancarlo Rostirolla (Palestrina: Fondazione Giovanni Pierluigi da Palestrina, 1991), 297–307.

21. "1 Mercoledì Santo si cantò la prima lamentaz[io]ne di Gregorio Allegri in Canto figurato à 4 voci, et il Miserere à 2 Chori del sud[et]to Autore. In questo giorno intervenne nel n[ost]ro Choro l'Altezza Serenis[si]ma del P[ri]nc[i]pe Alessandro figlio del Rè Giovanni di Polonia con la dispensa di N. S. con altre due in sua compagnia e molto applaudì il famoso concerto del sud[det]to Miserere." Biblioteca Apostolica Vaticana, Cappella Sistina, *Diario Sistino* 131 (1711), fol. 19r.

22. Ursula Kirkendale, "The Ruspoli Documents on Handel," in *Music and Meaning*, 298–99, 330, 375.

23. Ibid., 300, 303ff.

24. "Quindi ad istanza del collegio Tommaso Bai, di Crevalcuore nel Bolognese, maestro della basilica vaticana, scrisse nel 1714 un nuovo *Miserere* con un verso a 5 l'altro a 4 e l'ultimo a 8 voci sopra gli andamenti del *Miserere* dell'Allegri, ed avendo variato alcun poco, ma con chiarissime, semplicissime, ed insieme sublimi melodie anche gli altri versi, ottenne il massimo applauso, e perpetuò la sua gloria con questa sola produzione." Baini, *Memorie*, 196–97 n. 578.

25. "[Giovedì Santo] fù cantato il miserere del sig.r Thomaso Baij cantore della Basilica Vaticana, quale avendolo p[ri]ma presentato à N. S. si compiacque accettarlo, e lo mandò all'em[inentissim]o Protet[to]re; acciòche [sic] riconosciutolo al proposito, fosse fatto cantare, quale riuscì di commune applauso." Biblioteca Apostolica Vaticana, Cappella Sistina, *Diario Sistino* 131 (1711), fol. 20v.

26. Claudio Annibaldi, *La Cappella Musicale Pontificia nel Seicento, tomo primo: Da Urbano VII a Urbano VIII (1590–1644)*, Storia della Cappella musicale Pontificia, ed. Giancarlo Rostirolla (Palestrina: Fondazione Giovanni Pierluigi da Palestrina, 2011), 173 n. 37. I thank Claudio Annibaldi for sending me this volume prior to publication.

27. Ausilia Magaudda and Danilo Costantini, appendix to *Musica e spettacolo nel Regno di Napoli attraverso lo spoglio della «Gazzetta» (1675–1768)* (Rome: ISMEZ, 2011), 294.

28. Ralf Krause, "Das musikalische Panorama am neapolitanischen Hofe: Zur *Real Cappella di Palazzo* im frühen 18. Jahrhundert," in *Studien zur italienischen Musikgeschichte XV*, ed. Friedrich Lippmann, Analecta Musicologica, vol. 30, 271–95 (Laaber: Laaber-Verlag, 1998), 292 n. 114; Magaudda and Costantini, appendix to *Musica e spettacolo*, 191.

29. On a possible edition of the *Salve Regina* in 1697, see Scarlatti, *Concerti sacri*, xi–xii.

30. Poensgen refers to the year 1716 for the Salve Regina III and IV ("Offiziumskompositionen," 2:51, 52), but I have discovered archival sources regarding Scarlatti's appointment to "cavaliere" in July 1715, which make it clear that the summer of 1715 is the date in question; see Luca Della Libera, "Nuovi documenti biografici su Alessandro Scarlatti e la sua famiglia," *Acta Musicologica* 83, no. 2 (2011): 220–21.

31. Poensgen, "Offiziumskompositionen," 2:52.

32. All Roman numeral and scoring designations from Poensgen, "Offiziumskompositionen." The present edition uses the term "cantus" for the upper voices.

33. For a description of the manuscripts, see Poensgen, "Offiziumskompositionen," 2:19–21.

34. "Tra questi degni compositori merita al par d'ogn'altro una lode eterna il già nostro compagno Gregorio Allegri, il quale con poche note, ma sì ben modulate, e meglio intese hà composto il *Miserere*, che in tal giorno ogn'anno si canta, reso in vero la meraviglia de' nostri tempi, per esser concepito con proporzioni tali, che rapisce l'animo di chi l'ascolta," Adami, *Osservazioni per ben regolare il coro*, 37–38.

35. Unlike Allegri, Scarlatti did not set the first part of this versetto, "Tunc acceptabis sacrificium justitiae, oblationes, et holocausta."

36. The year of composition of of Allegri's *Miserere* is not known: see Julius Amann, *Allegris Miserere und die Aufführungspraxis in der Sixtina nach Reiseberichten und Musikhandschriften* (Regensburg: Verlag Friedrich Pustet, 1935), 27.

37. Magda Marx-Weber, "Römische Vertonungen," 13–14.

38. In some cases, there are minor rhythmic changes in the repetition of the same musical phrase.

39. See Marx-Weber, "Römische Vertonungen," 13.

40. Again, I have corrected Poensgen's date according to my recent findings: see note 30 above. An edition of the *Magnificat* I has long been announced by Hans-Jörg Jans and Benedikt Poensegn, in *I Vespri per Santa Cecilia di Alessandro Scarlatti e la Cappella di San Girolamo della Carità*, Musica Palatina (Libreria Musicale Italiana, forthcoming); see Poensgen, "Offiziumskompositionen," 2:28–31.

41. Jeanne Ellison Shaffer, "The cantus firmus in Alessandro Scarlatti's Motets" (Ph.D. diss., George Peabody College for Teachers, 1970), 324–29.

42. Ibid., 229, ex. 1. The plainchant melody transcribed by Shaffer is the alleluia verse for the Feast of the Immaculate Heart of Mary (22 August) that follows the gradual "Exsultavit cor meum"; see *Graduale Sacrosanctae Romanae Ecclesiae de Tempore et de Sanctis SS. D. N. Pii X. Pontificis Maximi Jussu Restitutum et editum* (Schwann: Düsseldorf, 1953), 235\*\*. For the first verset Scarlatti used material derived from the canticle; see *Graduale*, 263.

43. Ursula Kirkendale, *Antonio Caldara: Life and Venetian-Roman Oratorios* (Florence: Olschki, 2007), 253–54. J. S. Bach used this interval in the subject of the C-sharp minor fugue of the first book of the *Well-Tempered Clavier*.

44. Edward J. Dent, *Alessandro Scarlatti: His Life and Works*, new impression with preface and additional notes by Frank Walker (London: Edward Arnold, 1960), 136. See also Karl Gustav Fellerer, *Der Palestrinastil und seine Bedeutung in der vokalen Kirchenmusik des achtzehnten Jahrhunderts* (Augsburg: B. Filser Verlag, 1929), 118–20.

45. For a description of the manuscripts, see Dinko Fabris, *Music in Seventeenth-Century Naples: Francesco Provenzale (1624–1704)* (Aldershot: Ashgate, 2007), 95–97.

46. Ibid., 97.

47. Ibid., 97.

48. Schacht-Pape, *Messenschaffen*, 107–8.

49. Ibid., 111–12.

50. Della Libera, "Musica sacra," 157–58.

51. Ibid., 166–67.

52. The motet is preserved in the British Library, Add. 31508, fols. 66r–81r.

53. Bibioteca Apostolica Vaticana, *Diario Sistino* 128 (1708), fols. 2r–3r.

54. Ibid., fol. 44r.

55. Giancarlo Rostirolla, "Alcune note storico-istituzionali sulla Cappella Pontificia in relazione alla formazione e all'impiego dei repertori polifonici nel periodo post-palestriniano, fino a tutto il Settecento," in *Collectanea II*, 740 n. 569. See also Jean Lionnet, "Performance Practice in the Papal Chapel during the 17th Century," *Early Music* 15, no. 1 (1987): 3–15; Annibaldi, *Cappella Musicale Pontificia*, 250–54.

56. Adami, *Osservazioni per ben regolare il coro*, 36.

57. Ulisse Prota-Giurleo, "Breve storia del teatro di corte e della musica a Napoli nei secoli XVII–XVIII," in *Il Teatro di Corte del Palazzo Reale di Napoli*, ed. Felice de Filippis and Ulisse Prota-Giurleo (Naples: L'arte tipografica, 1952), 66.

58. Krause, "Musikalische Panorama," 274–75.

59. Francesco Cotticelli and Paologiovanni Maione, "Alessandro Scarlatti maestro di cappella a Napoli nel viceregno austriaco (1708–1725): Testimonianze inedite," *Studien zur italienischen Musikgeschichte XV*, 306–7.

60. Robert Donington, *The Intepretation of Early Music*, new rev. ed. (London: Faber & Faber, 1974), 386.

61. "Avverta pure il Signor Maestro che l'ultimo Verso del Salmo termina a due Cori, e però sarà la battuta adagio, per finirlo piano, smorzando a poco, a poco l'Armonia." Adami, *Osservazioni per ben regolare il coro*, 36.

62. "BATTUTA. veut dire, ce movement de la main, en *baissant* & en *levant*, qui sert à marquer la durée des Sons, & que nous apellons MESURE. On trouve souvent chez les Italiens ces mots *A battuta*, qui veulent dire de *Mesure*, on *en battant également* chaque temps. Ce qu'ils mettent ordinairement après, ce qu'il appellant *Recitativo*, qui est un chant où l'on *déclame* plûtôt qu'on ne *chante*, & dans lequel on n'observe Presque point la mesure. *A battuta* veut donc dire pour lors qu'il faut recommencer à marquer ou à batter *également* & juste tout les temps de la mesure." Sébastien de Brossard, *Dictionaire de musique, contenant une explication des Termes Grecs, Latins, Italiens, & François, les plus usitez dans la Musique* (1705; repr., Hilversum: Frits Knuf, 1965), 7.

63. "ADAGIO . . . veut dire proprement, COMMODEMENT, *à son aise, sans sa presser*, par consequent presque toûjours *lentement* & traînant un peu la Mesure." Brossard, *Dictionaire de musique*, xii, quoted in Donington, *Intepretation of Early Music*, 388.

64. "LARGO . . . VERY SLOW, as if enlarging the measure and making the main beats often inequal": Donington, *Intepretation of Early Music*, 388, quoting Brossard: "LARGO. veut dire, FORT LENTEMENT, comme en *élargissant* la mesure & marquant de *grands temps* souvent inégaux, etc. Ce qui arrive sur tout dans le *Recitativo* des Italiens, dans lequel souvent on ne fait pas les temps bien égaux, parce que c'est une espece de *declamation* où l'Acteur, doit suive plûtôt le movement de la passion qui l'agite ou qu'il veut exprimer, que celuy d'une mesure égalle & reglée." Brossard, *Dictionaire de musique*, 38.

65. http://www.ascarlatti2010.net/main_page/wdr3_1/

66. Alessandro Scarlatti, *Magnificat, Dixit Dominus, Madrigali*, with Rinaldo Alessandrini and Concerto Italiano, recorded in February 2000, Naïve, OP 30350, 2007, compact disc.

67. In Rome, additional continuo instrumentalists were only used in a few important feasts. See Tharald Borgir, *The Performance of the Basso Continuo in Italian Baroque Music* (UMI: Ann Arbor, 1987), 49–50.

Plate 1. Alessandro Scarlatti, *Salve Regina*, first page. Cambridge, Fitzwilliam Museum, Mu. Ms. 225, folio 9r. © The Fitzwilliam Museum, University of Cambridge.

Plate 2. Alessandro Scarlatti, *Miserere*, title page. Rome, Vatican Library, Capp. Sist. 188. © 2012 Biblioteca Apostolica Vaticana, reproduced courtesy of the Biblioteca Apostolica Vaticana, all rights reserved.

Plate 3. Alessandro Scarlatti, *Miserere*, Primus chorus, first page of music. Rome, Vatican Library, Capp. Sist. 188. © 2012 Biblioteca Apostolica Vaticana, reproduced courtesy of the Biblioteca Apostolica Vaticana, all rights reserved.

Plate 4. Alessandro Scarlatti, *Missa defunctorum*, first page. Bergamo, Biblioteca Donizetti, fondo Piatti-Lochis 9262, folio 1r. Courtesy of the Biblioteca Donizetti, Bergamo.

Plate 5. Alessandro Scarlatti, *Missa defunctorum*, Sequence, first page. Bergamo, Biblioteca Donizetti, fondo Piatti-Lochis 9262, folio 8v. Courtesy of the Biblioteca Donizetti, Bergamo.

# Salve Regina

15
-stra, spes no- - stra, sal- -
— spes no- stra, spes no- stra, sal- ve, sal-
— et — spes no- stra, sal- - ve, sal-
-stra, spes no- - stra, sal- - ve,
19
- - ve, sal- - -
-ve, sal- - ve, sal- -
- - ve, sal- -
sal- ve, sal- -
23
- ve, sal- - ve. Ad te, ad te cla- ma-
- ve, sal- - ve. Ad te cla- ma- -
-ve, sal- - ve. Ad te cla- ma- - mus, ad te
- ve, — sal- ve. Ad te cla- ma-

27
- mus, cla- ma- mus, ex-
- mus, cla- ma- mus, cla- ma- mus, ex-
cla- ma- - mus, cla- ma- mus, ex- - su- les,
- mus, cla- ma- mus, cla- ma- mus, ex- - su-
31
- su- les, ex- - su- les, fi- li- i,
- - - su- les, fi- li- i, fi-
ex- - - su- les, fi- li- i
-les, ex- - - su- les, fi- li- i
35
fi- li- i E- - - vae. Ad te su- spi- ra-
- li- i E- - - vae. Ad te su- spi- ra-
E- - - vae. Ad te su- spi- ra- mus,
E- - - vae. Ad

40
-mus, ad te su- - spi- ra- mus, ge- men- - tes,
-mus, ad te su- spi- ra- mus, ge- men- tes et
ad te su- spi- ra- mus, ge- men- - tes et
te su- spi- ra- mus, su- spi- ra- mus, ge- men- tes et flen-
44
ge- men- tes et flen- tes in hac
flen- tes, ge- men- tes et flen- - tes in hac la- cri-
flen- tes, ge- men- tes et flen- - tes
- tes, ge- men- tes et flen- tes
49
la- cri- ma- rum val- le, in hac la- cri- ma-
-ma- - rum val- le, in hac
in hac la- cri- ma- rum, in hac la- cri-
in hac la- cri- ma- - - rum val-

53
-rum, in hac lacri- ma- - rum val-
la- cri- ma- rum, in hac la- cri- ma- rum, in hac la- cri- ma- rum
-ma- rum val- le, in hac la- cri- ma- - rum val-
-le, in hac la- cri- ma- rum val-
57
- - le, sal- - -
val- - le, sal- - ve, sal-
- - le, sal- -
- - le, sal- -
61
-ve. E- ia er- go, ad- vo- ca- ta no- stra,
-ve. E- ia er- go, ad- vo- ca- ta no- - stra, e-
- ve. E- ia er- go, ad- vo- ca- ta no- stra, e- ia er-
-ve. E- ia er- go, ad- vo- ca- ta no- stra, e- ia

65
e- ia er- go, ad- vo- ca- ta no- - stra,
-ia er- go, ad- vo- ca- ta no- stra, il- los tu- os mi- se- ri-
-go, ad- vo- ca- ta no- - stra, il- los tu- os
er- go, e- ia er- go, ad- vo- ca- ta no- stra, il- los tu- os
69
il- los tu- os mi- se- ri- cor- des o-
-cor- des o- - cu- los, mi- se- ri- cor- des, mi- se- ri-
mi- se- ri- cor- des o- cu- los, il- los tu- os mi- se- ri- cor- des
mi- se- ri- cor- des o- cu- los, il- los tu- os mi- se- ri- cor- des
73
- cu- los ad nos con- ver- - te, ad nos con- ver-
-cor- des o- cu- los ad nos con- ver- - te, ad nos con- ver-
o- cu- los ad nos, ad nos con- ver- te, ad nos con- ver-
o- cu- los ad nos con- ver- - te, ad nos con-

77
- - te, sal- - ve, sal-
- te, con- ver- te, sal- -
- te, con- ver- te, sal- -
-ver- te, con- ver- te, sal-
81
- - ve, sal- - ve. Et Je-
- ve, sal- - ve. Et
-ve, sal- - - ve. Et
- ve, sal- - ve. Et
85
- sum, be- ne- di- ctum, be- ne- di- ctum fru- ctum, be-
Je- sum, be- - ne- di- ctum fru- ctum ven- tris tu-
Je- sum, be- ne- di- ctum, be- - ne- di- ctum fru- ctum
Je- sum, et Je- sum, be- ne- di- ctum fru- ctum, be- ne- di- ctum

88
- ne- di- ctum fru- ctum ven- - tris tu- i, no- bis post hoc ex- si- li- um
-i, ven- tris tu- i, no- bis post hoc ex- si-
ven- tris tu- i, no- bis post hoc ex- si- li- um
fru- ctum ven- tris tu- i, no- bis post hoc ex- si- li-
92
o- sten- - - - de,
- li- um o- sten- - de, o- sten- de,
o- sten- - - - de,
-um o- sten- - - de,
96
sal- - ve, sal- - ve, sal-
sal- - - ve, sal- - ve, sal-
sal- - ve, sal- - - ve, sal- -
sal- - ve, sal- - -

101
- - ve. O cle- - mens, o pi-
- - ve. O cle- - mens, o pi-
-ve, sal- - ve. o pi- - a,
- - ve. o pi-
106
- a, o cle- - mens, o pi- a,
- - a, o cle- - mens, o pi-
o cle- - mens, o pi-
-a, o cle- mens, o cle- mens, o
110
o pi- a, o dul- cis Vir- go Ma- ri-
- a, o dul- cis Vir- - go Ma- ri- a,
- a, o dul- cis Vir- go Ma- ri- -
pi- a, o dul- cis Vir- go Ma- ri-

114
-a, o cle- - mens, o pi- a, o dul- cis
o cle- - mens, o pi- a, o dul-
-a, o cle- - mens, o pi- a, o dul-
-a, o pi- - a, o
118
Vir- go Ma- ri- a, Ma- ri- a, o
-cis Vir- - go Ma- ri- a, o
- cis Vir- - go Ma- ri- a, o dul- cis
dul- cis Vir- go Ma- ri- a, o dul-
122
dul- cis Vir- go Ma- ri- a, Ma- ri- - a.
dul- cis Vir- go Ma- ri- a, Ma- ri- - a.
Vir- go, Vir- go Ma- - ri- a, Ma- ri- - a.
-cis Vir- go Ma- ri- a, Ma- ri- - a.

# Miserere

15
SECUNDUS CHORUS
C1
C2
A
T
B
Am- pli- us la- va me ab i- ni- qui- ta-
Am- pli- us la- va me ab i- ni- qui- ta-
Am- pli- us, am- pli- us la- va me ab i- ni- qui- ta-
Am- pli- us, am- pli- us la- va me ab i- ni- qui- ta-
Am- pli- us la- va me ab i- ni- qui- ta-
20
SECUNDUS CHORUS
C1
C2
A
T
B
- - te me- a: et a pec- ca- to
-te me- a: et a pec- ca- to
-te me- - a: et a pec- ca- to
-te me- - a: et a pec- ca- to
-te me- a: et a pec- ca- to
24
SECUNDUS CHORUS
C1
C2
A
T
B
me- o mun- da, mun- da me.
me- o mun- da, mun- da me.
me- o mun- da, mun- da, mun- da me.
me- o mun- da me, mun- - - da me.
me- o mun- da, mun- da me.

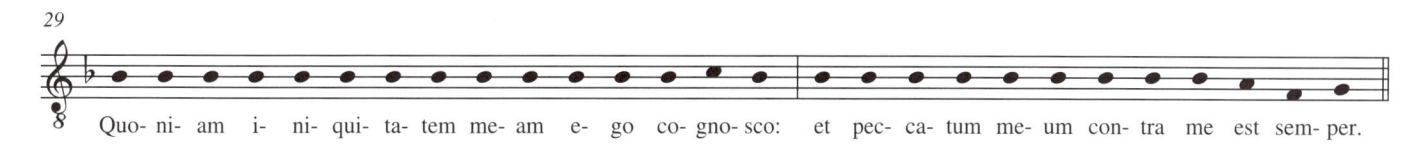

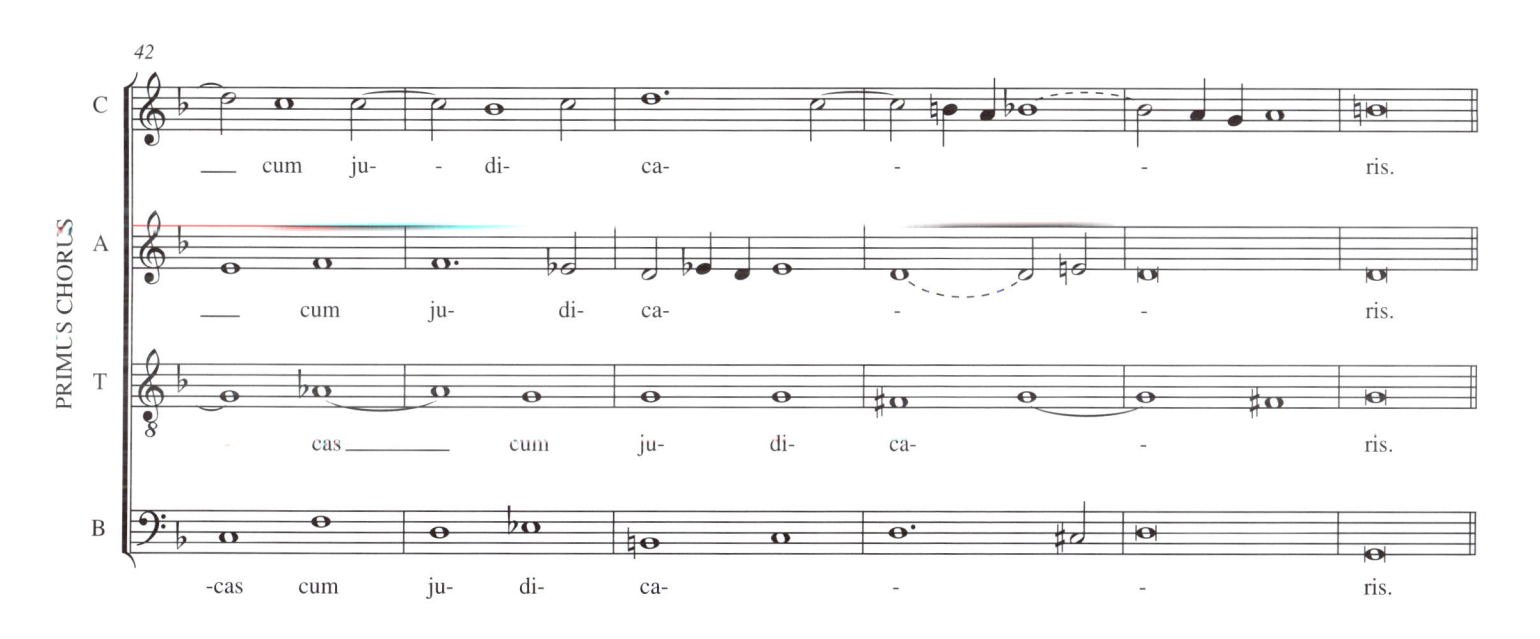

Quoniam iniquitatem meam ego cognosco: et peccatum meum contra me est semper.

Tibi soli peccavi, et malum coram te feci:

ut justificeris in sermonibus tuis, et vincas cum judicaris.

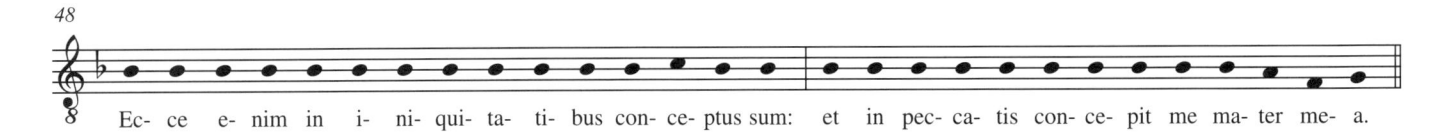

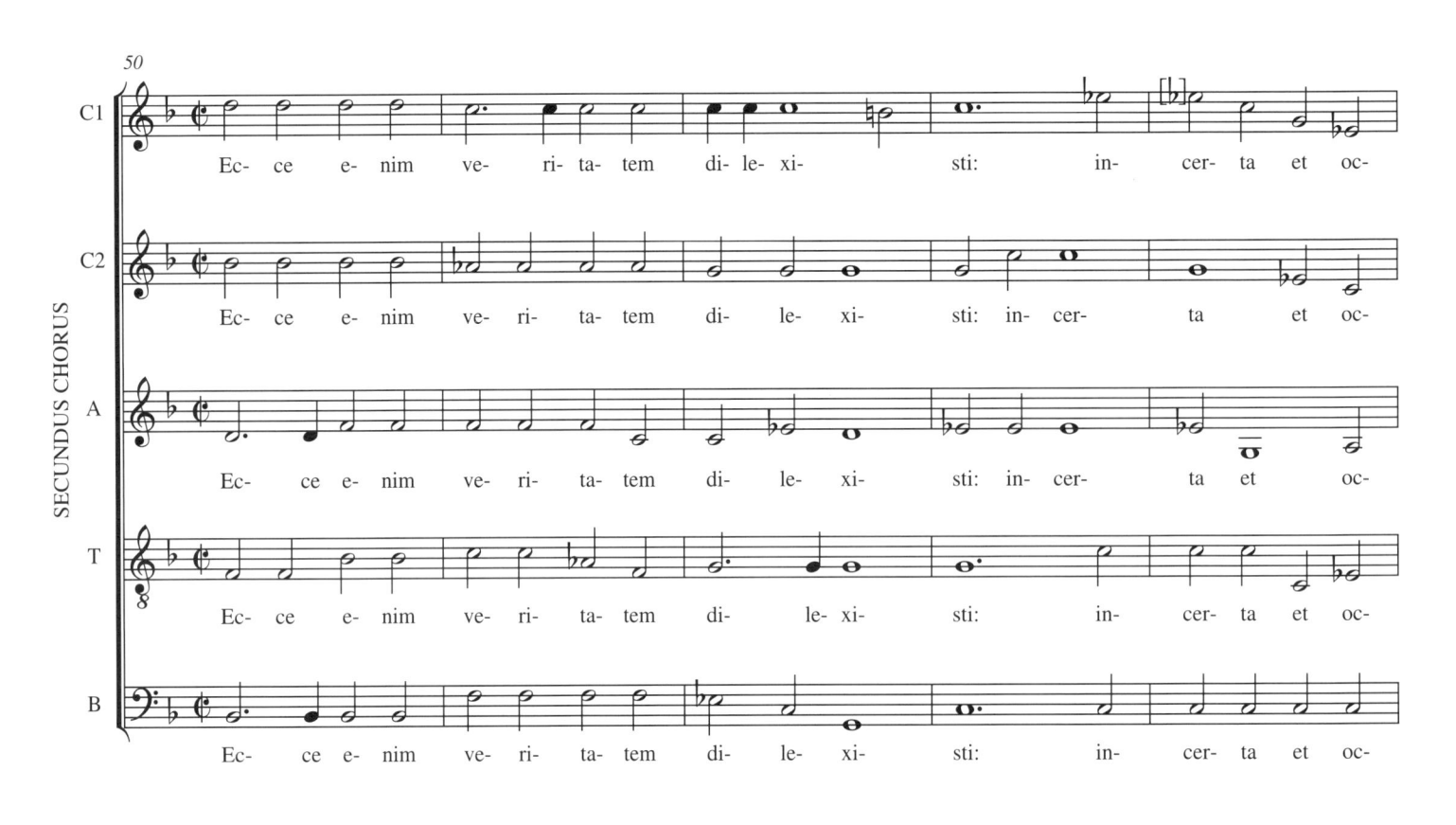

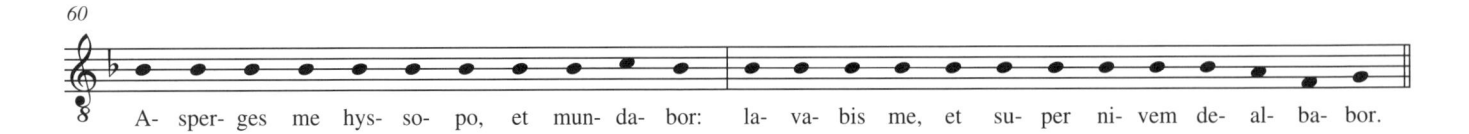

Ec- ce e- nim in i- ni- qui- ta- ti- bus con- ce- ptus sum: et in pec- ca- tis con- ce- pit me ma- ter me- a.

Ec- ce e- nim ve- ri- ta- tem di- le- xi- sti: in- cer- ta et oc- cul- ta sa- pi- en- ti- ae tu- ae ma- ni- fe- sta- sti mi- hi.

A- sper- ges me hys- so- po, et mun- da- bor: la- va- bis me, et su- per ni- vem de- al- ba- bor.

62
PRIMUS CHORUS
C
A
T
B
Au- di- tu- i me- o da- bis gau- di- um et lae- ti- ti- am:
Au- di- tu- i me- o da- bis gau- di- um et lae- ti- ti- am:
Au- di- tu- i me- o da- bis gau- di- um et lae- ti- - ti- am:
Au- di- tu- i me- o da- bis gau- di- um et lae- ti- ti- am:
67
PRIMUS CHORUS
et ex- sul- ta- bunt os- sa hu- mi- li- a- ta.
et ex- sul- ta- bunt os- sa hu- mi- li- - a- ta.
et ex- sul- ta- bunt os- sa hu- mi- li- a ta.
et ex- sul- ta- bunt os- sa hu- mi- li- a- ta.
72
A- ver- te fa- ci- em tu- am a pec- ca- tis me- is: et om- nes i- ni- qui- ta- tes me- as de- le.
74
SECUNDUS CHORUS
C1
C2
Cor mun- dum cre- a in me, De-
Cor mun- - dum cre- - a, cre- a in
Cor mun dum cre- - a, cre- a in
Cor mun- - dum cre- - a, cre- a in
Cor mun- dum cre- a in

79
C1
C2
A
T
B
SECUNDUS CHORUS
- - us: et spi- ri- tum re- ctum
me, De- us: et spi- - ri- tum re- ctum
me, De- - us: et spi- ri- tum re- ctum
me, De- - us: et spi- ri- tum re- ctum
me, De- us: et spi- ri- tum re- ctum
83
in- no- va in vi- sce- ri- bus me- is.
in- no- va in vi- sce- ri- bus me- is.
in- no- va in vi- sce- ri- bus, in vi- sce- ri- bus me- is.
in- no- va in vi- sce- ri- bus me- - - is.
in- no- va in vi- sce- ri- bus me- is.
88
Ne pro- ji- ci- as me a fa- ci- e tu- a: et spi- ri- tum san- ctum tu- um ne au- fe- ras a me.
90
PRIMUS CHORUS
Red- de mi- hi lae- ti- ti- am sa- - lu- ta- ris tu- i:
Red- de mi- hi lae- ti- ti- am sa- lu- ta- ris tu- i:
Red- de mi- hi lae- ti- ti- am sa- lu- ta- ris, sa- lu- ta- ris tu- - i:
Red- de mi- hi lae- ti- ti- am sa- lu- ta- ris, sa- - lu- ta- ris tu- i:

95
PRIMUS CHORUS
C
et spi- ri- tu prin- ci- pa- li con- fir- - ma me.
A
et spi- ri- tu prin- ci- pa- li con- fir- ma me.
T
et spi- ri- tu prin- ci- pa- li con- fir- ma me.
B
et spi- ri- tu prin- ci- pa- li con- fir- ma me.
100
Do- ce- bo i- ni- quos vi- as tu- as: et im- pi- i ad te con- ver- ten- tur.
102
SECUNDUS CHORUS
C1
Li- be- ra me de san- gui- ni- bus, De- us, De- us sa- lu- tis
C2
Li- be- ra me de san- gui- ni- bus, De- us, De- us sa- lu- tis
A
Li- be- ra me de san- gui- ni- bus, De- us, De- us sa- lu- tis me-
T
Li- be- ra me de san- gui- ni- bus, De- us, De- us sa- lu- tis
B
Li- be- ra me de san- gui- ni- bus, De- us, De- us sa- lu- tis
107
SECUNDUS CHORUS
C1
me- ae: et ex- sul- ta- bit lin-gua me- a ju- sti- - ti- am tu- am.
C2
me- ae: et ex- sul- ta- bit lin-gua me- a ju- sti- - ti- am tu- - am.
A
-ae: et ex sul ta bit lin gua me- a ju- sti- ti- am tu- am.
T
me- ae: et ex- sul- ta- bit lin-gua me- a ju- sti- ti- am tu- am.
B
me- ae: et ex- sul- ta- bit lin- gua me- a ju- sti- ti- am tu- am.

112
Do- mi- ne, la- bi- a me- a a- pe- ri- es: et os me- um an- nun- ti- a- bit lau- dem tu- am.
114
PRIMUS CHORUS
C
Quo- ni- am si vo- lu- is- - ses sa- cri- fi- ci- um, de- dis- sem u-
A
Quo- ni- am si vo- - lu- is- ses sa- cri- fi- ci- um, de- dis- sem
T
Quo- ni- am si vo- - lu- is- ses sa- cri- fi- ci- um, de- dis- sem
B
Quo- ni- am si vo- lu- is- ses sa- cri- fi- ci- um, de- dis- sem u-
119
PRIMUS CHORUS
C
- ti- que: ho- lo- cau- stis, ho- lo- cau- - stis non
A
u- ti- que: ho- lo- cau- stis, ho- lo- cau- - stis non de-
T
u- ti- que: ho- lo- cau- stis, ho- lo- cau- - stis non de-
B
- ti- que: ho- lo- cau- stis, ho- lo- cau- stis non de- le- cta- be-
125
PRIMUS CHORUS
C
de- le- cta- - - - - be- ris.
A
- le- cta- - - - be- ris.
T
- le- - cta- - be- ris, non de- le- cta- - be- ris.
B
-ris, non de- le- cta- - - be- ris.

Sa- cri- fi- ci- um De- o spi- ri- tus con- tri- bu- la- tus: cor con- tri- tum et hu- mi- li- a- tum, De- us, non de- spi- ci- es.

**SECUNDUS CHORUS**

C1: Be- ni- gne fac, Do- mi- ne, in
C2: Be- ni- gne fac, Do- mi- ne, in bo- na
A: Be- ni- gne fac, Do- mi- ne, in bo- na vo- lun- ta-
T: Be- ni- gne fac, Do- mi- ne, in bo- na vo- lun-
B: Be- ni- gne fac, Do- mi- ne, in bo- na

C1: bo- na vo- lun- ta- te tu- a Si- on: ut ae- di- fi- cen-
C2: vo- lun- ta- te tu- a Si- on: ut ae- di- fi- cen-
A: -te tu- a Si- on: ut ae- di- fi- cen-
T: -ta- te tu- a Si- on: ut ae- di- fi-
B: vo- lun- ta- te tu- a Si- on: ut ae- di- fi-

Tunc acceptabis sacrificium justitiae, oblationes et holocausta:

152
PRIMUS CHORUS
C
tu- um vi- - tu- los.
A
tu- um vi- - tu- los.
T
-um vi- - tu- los.
B
tu- um vi- - - tu- los.
SECUNDUS CHORUS
C1
-re tu- um vi- - - tu- los.
C2
- re tu- um vi- tu- los, vi- tu- los.
A
- re tu- um vi- - tu- los.
T
-re tu- um vi- - tu- los.
B
-re tu- um vi- - tu- los.

# Magnificat

11
C1
-ni-ma me- a Do- mi-num, a- ni-ma
C2
ma- gni- fi- cat a- ni-ma me- a Do- -mi- num,
A
-a, ma- gni- fi- cat a- ni-ma me- a Do- -mi- num, Do-
T
me- a Do- mi-num, ma- gni- fi- cat a- -ni-ma Do- mi- num, a-
B
-gni- fi- cat a- -ni-ma me- a Do- mi-num, Do- -mi-num,
16
C1
me- a Do- - mi- num, ma- gni- fi- cat a- -ni-ma me-
C2
a- ni-ma me- a Do- mi- num,
A
- -mi-num, a- ni-ma me- a Do- -
T
-ni-ma me- - a Do- -mi- num, a- ni-ma
B
ma- gni- fi- cat a- ni-ma me- a

24

29
C1
Et ex- sul- ta- - -
C2
- - - vit,
A
- - -
T
-ta- - -
B
Et ex- sul- ta-
32
C1
- vit,
C2
et ex- sul- ta- -
A
- - -
T
- - -
B
- - - vit,

35
C1
C2
A
T
B
et ex- sul- ta- -
- - -
- vit, et ex- sul- ta-
- - vit, et ex- sul-
et ex- sul- ta- - -
38
- vit spi- ri- tus me- us in De- o
- vit spi- ri- tus me- us in De- o
- vit spi- ri- tus me- us in De- o
-ta- - vit spi- ri- tus me- us
- - vit spi- ri- tus me- us

42
C1
sa- lu- ta- ri me- o, in De- o sa- lu- ta- ri me- o, in De- o sa- lu- ta-
C2
sa- lu- ta- ri me- o, in De- o sa- lu- ta- ri me- o, in De- o sa- lu- ta-
A
sa- lu- ta- ri me- o, in De- o sa- lu- ta- ri me- o, in De- o sa- lu- ta-
T
in De- o sa- lu- ta- ri me- o, in De- o sa- lu- ta-
B
in De- o sa- lu- ta- ri me- o,
47
C1
-ri me- o, in De- o sa- lu- ta- ri me- - o.
C2
-ri me- o, in De- o sa- lu- ta- ri me- - o.
A
-ri me- o, in De- o sa- lu- ta- ri me- - o.
T
-ri me- o, in De- o sa- lu- ta- ri me- o.
B
in De- o sa- lu- ta- ri me- o.

Largo
solo
C1
Qui- a re- spe- xit hu- mi- li- ta- tem, hu- mi- li- ta-
-tem an- cil- lae su- - ae, hu- mi- li-
-ta- tem an- cil- lae su- ae, an- cil- lae su- - ae:
ec- ce e- nim ex hoc be- a- - tam me di- cent om- nes ge- ne- ra-
C2
om- nes ge- ne- ra-
A
om- nes
T
om- nes ge- ne- ra-
B
om- nes ge- ne- ra-

68
C1
- ti- o- nes, om- nes ge- ne- ra- - ti- o- nes,
C2
- ti- o- nes, om- nes ge- ne- ra- - ti- o- nes,
A
ge- ne- ra- ti- o- nes, om- nes ge- ne- ra- ti- o- nes,
T
- ti- o- nes, om- nes ge- ne- ra- ti- o- nes,
B
- ti- o- nes, om- nes ge- ne- ra- - ti- o- nes,
72
C1
om- nes ge- ne- ra- - ti- o- nes, om- nes ge- ne- ra- ti- o- nes.
C2
om- nes ge- ne- ra- - ti- o- nes, om- nes ge- ne- ra- ti- o- nes.
A
om- nes ge- ne- ra- ti- o- nes, om- nes ge- ne- ra- ti- o- nes.
T
om- nes ge- ne- ra- - ti- o- nes, om- nes ge- ne- ra- ti- o- nes.
B
om- nes ge- ne- ra- - ti- o- nes, om- nes ge- ne- ra- ti- o- nes.

C1
Qui- a fe-cit mi-hi ma- gna,__ qui po- -
- tens est, qui- a fe- cit mi- hi ma- gna,__
qui po- - - tens
est, qui po- - - tens
est: et san-ctum no-men e- - jus,__ et san-ctum no-men e-
- jus, et san-ctum no- men e- jus,__ et san- ctum no- men e- jus,__

95
C1
no- - men e- jus, et san- ctum
98
C1
C2
A
T
B
no- men e- jus. Et mi- se- ri- cor- di- a e- jus a pro- ge- ni- e
Et mi- se- ri- cor- di- a e- jus a pro- ge- ni- e
102
in pro- ge- ni- es ti- men- - ti- bus e- um,
in pro- ge- ni- es ti- men- - ti- bus e- um, ti- men- - ti- bus e-
in pro- ge- ni- es ti- men- - ti- bus e- um, ti- men- - ti- bus e-
in pro- ge- ni- es ti- men- - ti- bus e- um, ti- men- - ti- bus e-
in pro- ge- ni- es ti- men- - ti- bus e- um,

107
C1
et mi- se- ri- cor- di- a e- jus a pro- ge- ni- e in pro- ge- ni- es ti-
C2
-um, et mi- se- ri- cor- di- a e- jus a pro- ge- ni- e in pro- ge- ni- es ti-
A
-um, et mi- se- ri- cor- di- a e- jus a pro- ge- ni- e in pro- ge- ni- es ti-
T
-um, et mi- se- ri- cor- di- a e- jus a pro- ge- ni- e in pro- ge- ni- es ti-
B
et mi- se- ri- cor- di- a e- jus a pro- ge- ni- e in pro- ge- ni- es ti-
♮6 6 7 6 ♯ 6 [7 ♮6]
112
C1
-men- ti- bus e- um, ti- men- ti- bus e- - um.
C2
-men- ti- bus e- um, ti- men- ti- bus e- - um.
A
-men- ti- bus e- um, ti- men- ti- bus e- - um.
T
-men- ti- bus e- um, ti- men- ti- bus e- - um.
B
-men- ti- bus e- um, ti- men- ti- bus e- - um.
♯ 4 ♯ ♯ ♮ ♯ 6 4 [5] ♯ ♯

33

128
C1
in brachi-o su- o, in brachi-o su- o: di- sper- sit, di- sper- sit,
A
su- o, in brachi-o su- o, su- o: di- sper- sit, di- sper-
T
brachi-o su- o, in brachi-o su- o: di- sper- sit, di- sper-
132
C1
di- sper- - sit super- bos, super- bos, di-
A
-sit super- bos, di- sper- sit, di- sper- - sit, di- sper-
T
-sit, di- sper- - sit, di- sper- sit, di- sper- - sit, di- sper-
136
C1
-sper- sit, di- sper- - sit su- per- bos, su- per-
A
- sit, di- sper- - sit, di- sper- sit su- per- bos, su- per-
T
- sit su- per- bos, di- sper- - sit su- per- bos, su- per-

35

153
C1
- tes, po- - ten- - tes, de- po-
C2
- - - su- it
A
- tes, de- po- - su- it,
T
de- po- - - su- it, de- po- -
B
-tes, de- po- - - su- it po- ten- tes, de- po-
9 8 4 ♯ 6 ♮
158
C1
- - su- it po- ten- tes, po- ten- - tes, po- ten-
C2
po- - ten- tes de
A
de- po- su- it po- ten- tes, po- ten- tes
T
- su- it po- ten- tes, po- - ten- tes
B
- su- it po- ten- tes, po- ten- tes, po- ten- tes de
9 8 4 ♯ ♮ ♮ ♭

163
C1
-tes de se- de, et ex- al- ta- vit, et ex- al- ta-
C2
se- - de, et
A
de se- de, de se- de, et ex- al- ta- vit, et ex- al-
T
de se- - de, et ex- al- ta- vit, et ex- al- ta- vit, et
B
se- - de, et ex-
5
167
C1
-vit, et ex- al- ta- vit, et ex- al- ta- vit, et ex- al- ta- vit, et ex- al- ta- vit, et ex- al-
C2
ex- al- ta- vit
A
ta vit, et ex- al- ta- - vit, et ex- al- ta- vit, et ex- al- ta- vit, et
T
ex- al- ta- vit, et ex- al- ta- vit, et ex- al- ta- vit, et ex- al- ta- vit, et ex- al- ta-
B
-al- ta- - vit, et ex- al- ta- vit, et
5
5

171
C1
-ta- vit, et ex- al- ta- vit, et ex- al- ta- vit, et ex- al- - ta- vit, et
C2
hu- - -
A
ex- al- ta- vit, et ex- al- ta- vit, et ex- al- ta- vit, et ex- al- ta-
T
-vit, et ex- al- ta- vit, et ex- al- ta- vit, et ex- al- ta- vit, et ex- al- ta-
B
ex- al- ta- vit, et ex- al- ta-
♭ 6 5
175
C1
ex- al- ta- - vit hu- mi- les, et ex- al- ta-
C2
- - mi- les.
A
-vit, et ex- al- ta- vit hu- - mi- les, et ex- al-
T
- vit, et ex- al- ta- vit hu- mi- les, et ex- al- ta-
B
-vit, ex- al- ta- vit hu- mi- les, et
♯ 6 4 [5] [♯] ♯

179
C1
-vit, et ex- al- ta- vit hu- - - mi- les.
C2
A
-ta- vit hu- - mi- les.
T
-vit, et ex- - al- ta- vit hu- mi- les.
B
ex- al- ta- vit hu- - mi- les.
184
a 3
C1
E- su- ri- en- tes im- ple- vit bo- nis, im- ple-
C2
E- su- ri- en- tes im- ple- vit bo- nis,___ im- ple-
T
E- su- ri- en- - tes im- ple- - vit bo- nis, im- ple-
188
C1
- - vit bo- nis, e- su- ri- en- tes im- ple-
C2
- - vit bo- nis,___ e- su- ri- en- tes im- ple-
T
- - vit bo- nis, e- su- ri- en- tes im- ple-

192
C1
- - vit bo- nis: et di- vi-tes di- mi-
C2
- - vit bo- nis: et di- vi- tes di- mi- sit i-
T
- - vit bo- nis: et di- vi- tes di- mi- - sit i- na-
196
C1
- sit i- na- nes, et di- vi- tes di- mi- sit, et di- vi- tes di- mi-
C2
-na- nes, et di- vi- tes di- mi- sit i-
T
- nes, et di- vi- tes di- mi- - sit i- na- -
200
C1
- sit i- na- nes, et di- vi- tes di- mi- sit i- na- nes. Su- sce-
C2
-na- nes, et di- vi- tes di- mi- - sit, di- mi- sit i- na- nes. Su-
T
- nes, et di- vi- tes di- mi- sit, di- mi- sit i- na- nes. Su-

204
C1
C2
T
-pit Is- -ra- el, su- sce- pit Is- -ra- el pu-
-sce- pit Is- -ra- el, su- sce- -pit Is- -ra- el
-sce- pit Is- -ra- el, su- sce- pit Is- -ra- el
208
-e- rum su- um, pu- -e rum su um, pu- e- rum su- um, su-
pu- e- rum su- um, pu- e- rum su- -
pu- e- rum su- -um, pu- e- rum
213
-um: mi- se- ri- cor- di- ae su-
-um: mi- se- ri- cor- di- ae su- -ae,
su- um: re- -cor- da- -tus mi-

218
C1
-ae, re- cor- da- tus mi- se- ri-
C2
re- cor- da- - tus mi- se- ri- cor- di- ae
T
-se- ri- cor- di- ae, mi- se- ri- cor- di- ae su- ae,
223
C1
-cor- di- ae su- ae, re- - cor- da- - tus
C2
su- ae, mi- se- ri- cor- di- ae, re- cor- da-
T
mi- se- ri- cor- di- ae su- - ae, re- cor-
228
C1
mi- se- ri- cor- di- ae su- ae, re- cor-
C2
- tus mi- se- ri- cor- di- ae su- ae, re-
T
-da- tus mi- se- ri- cor- di- ae su- ae, re-

233
C1
-da- - tus mi- se- ri- cor- di- ae su-
C2
- cor- da- - tus mi- se- ri- cor- di-
T
- cor- da- - tus mi- se- ri- cor- di- ae su- - ae,
238
C1
- - ae, mi- se- ri- cor- di- ae,
C2
-ae su- - ae, mi- se- ri- cor- di- ae su- -
T
mi- se- ri- cor- di- ae su- ae, re- cor-
243
C1
mi- se- ri- cor- di- ae, re- cor- da- -
C2
- ae, mi- se- ri- cor- di- ae su- - -
T
-da- - tus mi- se- ri- cor- - di- ae, mi- se- ri- cor- di-

248
C1
- - tus mi- se- ri- cor- di- ae,
C2
- ae, re- cor- da- tus mi-
T
-ae su- - ae, mi- se- ri- cor- di- ae su-
253
C1
mi- se- ri- cor- di- ae su- - ae.
C2
-se- ri- cor- di- ae su- - - ae.
T
- ae, su- - ae, su- - ae.
258
C1
Sic- ut lo- cu- tus est ad pa- tres no- stros, sic- ut lo- cu- tus
C2
⟨Sic- ut lo- cu- tus est ad pa- tres no- stros,⟩ sic- ut lo- cu- tus
A
⟨Sic- ut lo- cu- tus⟩ est ad pa- tres no- stros, sic- ut lo- cu- tus
T
⟨Sic- ut lo- cu- tus est ad pa- tres no- stros,⟩ sic- ut lo- cu- tus
B
Sic- ut lo- cu- tus est ad pa- tres no- stros,

262
C1
est ad pa- tres no- stros, A- bra-ham et se- mi- ni e- jus
C2
est ad pa- tres no- stros, A- bra-ham et se- mi- ni e- jus
A
est ad pa- ⟨tres no- stros,⟩ A- bra- ham et se- mi- ni e- jus
T
est ad pa- ⟨tres no- stros,⟩ A- bra-ham,
B
A- bra-ham et se- mi- ni e- jus
4 ♯ ♭6 ♭

266
C1
in sae- cu- la, A- bra-ham, A- bra-ham, A- bra-ham
C2
in sae- cu- la, A- bra-ham, A- bra-ham, A- bra-ham
A
in sae- cu- la, A- bra- ham, A- bra-ham, A- bra-ham
T
A- - bra-ham, A- bra-ham, A- bra-ham
B
in sae- cu- la, A- bra-ham, A- bra-ham
♭ 4 ♯ [♭] [♮]

270
C1
C2
A
T
B
et se- mi- ni e- jus in sae- cu- la,
⟨et se- mi- ni e- jus in sae- cu- la,
et se- mi- ni e- jus in sae- cu- la,
et se- mi- ni e- jus — in sae- cu- la,
274
solo
et se- mi- ni e- jus in sae- cu- la.
Glo- ri-
et se- mi- ni e- jus in sae- cu- la.⟩
et se- mi- ni e- jus ⟨in sae- cu- la.⟩
et se- mi- ni e- jus in sae- cu- la.

C1
-a, glo- - -
C2
ri- a Pa- tri,
Glo- - -
- ri- a Pa- tri,
et Fi- - li- o, et
et Fi- - li- o, et Fi-
A
T
B
et Fi- li- o, et Fi- - li- o, et
et Fi- li- o, et
et Fi- li- o, et

*The continuo part from here to the end of the piece is editorial with the exception of m. 308, note 2, and m. 309, note 1.

297
C1
nunc, et sem- - - -
C2
- - - - per,
A
- - per, et nunc, et sem- -
T
Sic- ut e- rat in prin- ci- pi- o, et nunc, et sem-
B
Sic- ut e- rat in prin- ci- pi-
7 ♯6 7 ♯6
301
C1
-per, sic- ut e- rat in prin- ci- pi- o, et nunc, et sem- per,
C2
et nunc, et sem- per, sic- ut e- rat in prin-
A
-per, et nunc, et sem- -
T
- - - per, et
B
-o, et nunc, et sem- - -
6 6 6 6 6

305
C1
C2
A
T
B
et nunc, et sem- - -
-ci- pi- o, et nunc, et sem- -
- per, sic- ut e- rat in prin- ci- pi-
nunc, et sem- - per, sic-
- - - -
309
-per, sic- ut e- rat in prin- ci- pi- o, et nunc, et
- - - - per,
-o, et nunc, et sem- - per, et
- ut e- rat in prin- ci- pi- o, et nunc, et sem-
-per, et nunc, et sem- - - per,

313
C1
sem- - per, et nunc, et
C2
et nunc, et sem- per,
A
nunc, et sem- - per, et nunc, et sem-
T
- per, et nunc, et sem- -
B
sic- ut e- rat in prin- ci- pi- o, et nunc, et sem-
317
C1
sem- - - -
C2
sic- ut e- rat in prin- ci- pi- o, et nunc, et sem-
A
- - per,
T
- per, et nunc, et sem- -
B
- - per, sic- ut

321
C1
C2
A
T
B
- - per, sic- ut e- rat in prin- ci- pi-
- - - per, et nunc, et
sic- ut e- rat in prin- ci- pi- o, et nunc,
- - - -
e- rat in prin- ci- pi- o, et nunc, et sem- -
7 ♯6 6 6

325
C1
C2
A
T
B
-o, et nunc, et sem-
sem- - - per,
et sem- - - per, sem-
- per, sic- ut e- rat in prin- ci- pi- o, et nunc, et
- - - per, et nunc, et sem-
♯6 6 4 ♯ ♯ 6

329
C1
C2
sic- ut e- rat in prin- ci- pi- o, et
A
per, et nunc, et sem-
T
sem- per,
B

333
C1
-per, et nunc, et sem-
C2
nunc, et sem- per, et nunc, et sem-
A
per, sic- ut e- rat
T
sic- ut e- rat in prin- ci- pi- o, et nunc, et sem-
B
per, sic- ut e- rat in prin- ci- pi-

337
C1
- ⟨per,⟩ sic- ut e- rat in prin-
C2
-per, et nunc, et sem-
A
in prin- ci- pi- o, et nunc, et sem- - per,
T
- - - per, et nunc, et sem-
B
-o, sic- ut e- rat in prin- ci- pi- o, et nunc, et
341
C1
-ci- pi- o, et nunc, et sem- - -
C2
-per, sic- ut e- rat in prin- ci- pi- o, et nunc, et
A
et nunc, et sem- - -
T
- - per, et
B
sem- - - -

345
C1
C2
A
T
B
- - per, et in sae- - cu- la
sem- - per, et in sae- - cu- la
- - per, et in sae- - cu- la
nunc, et sem- - per, et in sae- - cu- la
- - per, et in sae- - cu- la
349
sae- cu- lo- rum, a- men, et in sae- - cu- la
sae- cu- lo- rum, a- men, et in sae- - cu- la
sae- cu- lo- rum, a- men, et in sae- - cu- la
sae- cu- lo- rum, a- men, et in sae- - cu- la
sae- cu- lo- rum, a- men, et in sae- cu- la

352
C1
sae- cu- lo- rum, a- men, et in sae- - cu- la
C2
sae- cu- lo- rum, a- men, et in sae- - cu- la
A
sae- cu- lo- rum, a- men, et in sae- - cu- la
T
sae- cu- lo- rum, a- men, et in sae- - cu- la
B
sae- cu- lo- rum, a- men, et in sae- cu- la
355
C1
sae- cu- lo- rum, a- men, sae- cu- lo- rum, a- men.
C2
sae- cu- lo- rum, a- men, sae- cu- lo- rum, a- men.
A
sae- cu- lo- rum, a- men, sae- cu- lo- rum, a- men. A-
T
sae- cu- lo- rum, a- men, sae- cu- lo- rum, a- men.
B
sae- cu- lo- rum, a- men, sae- cu- lo- rum, a- men.

359
C1
C2
A
T
B
A-
A- - - - -
- - - - - men,
A- -
A- - -
7 ♯6 7 6 7 ♯6 4 ♯
364
- - men, a-
- men, a- -
a- - -
- - men, a- - - -
- - men, a- - - men,
7 6 ♭ ♭7 6 7 7 ♯6 4 ♯ 6

369
C1
men,
C2
A
men, a-
T
men, a- men,
B
a-
7 ♯6 4 ♯ ♭ ♭6 2 6 5 6 5 ♯ 7 6 ♯6
374
C1
a-
C2
men, a-
A
T
a- men, a-
B
men, a-
7 ♯6 ♯ ♯6 6 6 5 ♯

59

388
C1
a- - - men, a- -
C2
- - men, a- - -
A
- - - - men,
T
- - - men, a-
B
a- - - men,
2 6 5 4 ♯ 7 6 7 ♯6
393
C1
- - men, a- -
C2
- - - men,
A
a- - men, a-
T
- men, a- -
B
a- - - -
2 6 4 ♯ 7 6

61

62

# Missa defunctorum

## Introit

15
lu- ce- at e- - is, et lux per- pe- tu- a, et
-a lu- ce- at e- is, et lux per- pe- tu- a, et lux
- ce- at e- - is, et lux per- pe- tu- a, et lux per-
-a lu- ce- at e- is, et lux per-
20
lux per- pe- tu- a lu- ce- at e- is, et lux per- pe- - tu- a
lu- ce- at e- is, et lux per- pe- tu- a lu- ce- at
-pe- tu- a lu- - ce- at e- is, et lux per- pe- tu- a lu- ce-
-pe- tu- a, lu- - ce- at e- is, et lux per- pe- - tu- a
25
lu- ce- - at e- is, lu- ce- at e- is.
e- - is, lu- - ce- at e- - is.
-at e- is, lu- ce- at e- - is.
lu- ce- at e- is, lu- ce- at e- is.

[Fine]

30
Te de- cet hym- nus De- us in Si-
Te de- cet hym- nus De- us in Si-
Te de- cet hym- nus De- us in Si-
35
-on, te de- cet hym- nus De- us
-on, te de- cet hym- nus De- us in Si-
-on, te de- cet hym- nus De- us, De- us in
Te de- cet hym- nus, te de- cet hym- nus De- us in Si-
40
et ti- bi red- de- tur vo- tum in Je- ru- sa-
on, in Je- ru- sa- lem, et ti- bi red- de- tur
Si- on, et ti- bi red- de- tur vo- tum in
on, et ti- bi red- de- tur vo- tum

45
- lem, in Je- ru- sa- lem: ex- au- di o-
vo- tum in Je- ru- - sa- lem: ex- au-
Je- ru- sa- lem, in Je- ru- sa- lem: ex- au-
in Je- ru- sa- lem: ex- au-
6 6 4 ♮ 7 5 6 6 5 6 4 [5] 3 ♭
50
-ra- ti- o- nem, ex- au- di o- ra- ti- o- nem me-
-di o- ra- ti- o- nem, ex- au- di o- ra- ti- o- - nem me-
-di o- ra- ti- o- nem, ex- au- di o- ra- ti- o- nem me-
-di o- ra- ti- o- nem, ex- au- di o- ra- ti- o- nem me-
♭6 ♭ 6 5 3 ♭6 4 [5] 3
55
-am, ad te om- nis ca- ro ve- ni- et,
-am, ad te om- nis ca- ro ve- - ni- et,
-am, ad te om- nis ca- ro
-am, ad te om- nis
[♭] ♭ ♮ 7 ♯ ♭ 6 ♭6 ♮4 2 6

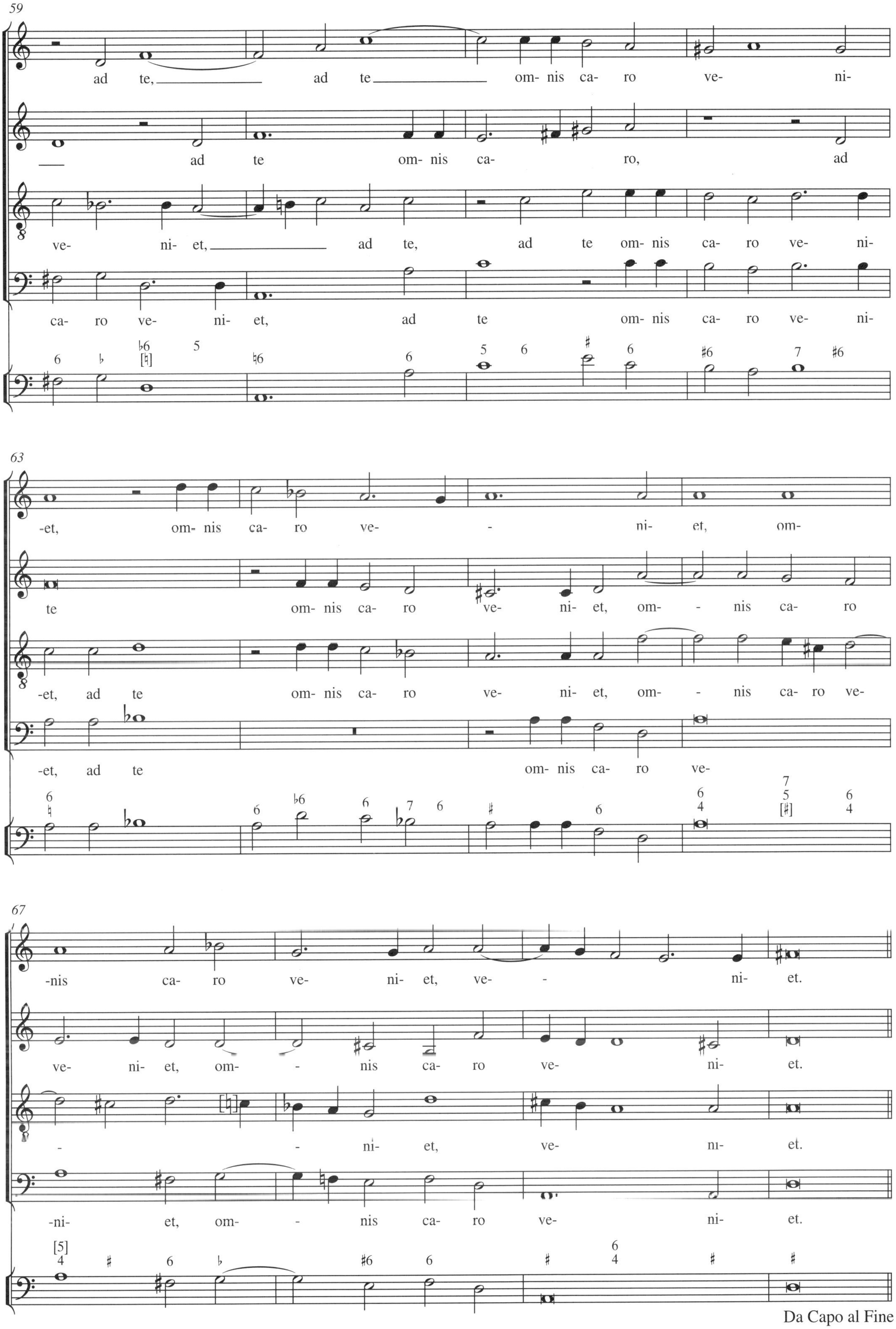


Da Capo al Fine

# Kyrie

13
- ste e- le- - - i- son, Chri- ste
e- le- - - i- son, Chri-
-ste e- le- - - i- son, e- le-
-le- - - i- son, Chri- ste e-
17
e- le- - - i- son, Ky- ri- e
-ste e- le- - - i- son, Ky- ri- e
- - i- son, Ky- ri- e
-le- - i- son,
21
e- le- - - i- son, Ky- ri- e e-
e- le- - - i- son, Ky- ri- e
e- le- - i- son, e- le-
Ky- - ri- e, Ky- ri-

25
-le- - - i- son, Ky- ri-
e- le- - - i- son, e- le-
- - - i- son, Ky- ri- e
-e e- le- - - i- son, e- le-
29
-e e- le- - i- son, Ky- ri- e e-
- i- son, Ky- ri- e, Ky- - ri- e
e- le- i- son, Ky- ri- e, Ky- ri- e
- i- son, Ky- ri- e e- le-
33
-le- - i- son, e- le- i- son.
e- le- - - i- son, e- lei- son.
e- le- - i- son, e- le- - i- son.
- i- son, e- le- i- son.

# Gradual

16
- is, et lux per- pe- tu- a, et lux per- pe- tu-
e- is, et lux per- pe- tu- a, et lux lu- ce-
- is, et lux per- pe- tu- a, et lux per- pe- tu- a lu-
e- is, et lux per- pe- tu- a lu-
♯ 6 7 ♯6 6 6 [6]
21
-a lu- ce- at e- is, et lux per- pe- - tu- a lu- ce-
-at e- is, et lux per- pe- tu- a lu- ce- at e-
- ce- at e- is, et lux per- pe- tu- a lu- ce- at e-
- ce- at e- is, et lux per- pe- - tu- a lu- ce- at
6 ♯ 7 6 ♯ 6 4 [5] 4 ♯ ♮6 4 [5] ♯ ♯ 6 5 6 4 ♯ 7 6
26
- at e- is, lu- ce- at e- is.
- is, lu- - ce- at e- - is.
-is, lu- ce- at e- - is. In me- mo-
e- is, lu- ce- at e- is. In me- mo- ri-
7 ♮6 5 6 7 ♯ 6 4 [5] ♯ ♯

31
In memo- ri- a ae- ter- na e- rit ju- - stus,
In me- mo- - ri- a ae- ter- na e- rit ju- stus, in
- ri- a ae- ter- na e- rit ju- stus, in me- mo- ri-
-a ae- ter- na e- rit ju- stus, e- rit ju- - stus, in
6 ♮ ♮ 5 6 [6] 6 7 ♯6 ♮6
35
in me- mo- ri- a ae- ter- na e- rit ju-
me- mo- ri- a ae- ter- na e- rit ju- stus, ju-
-a, in me- mo- ri- a ae- ter- na e- rit, e- rit ju-
me- mo- ri- a ae- ter- na e- rit ju- stus, e- - rit ju-
[5] 6 [6] 4 3 6 ♮ ♮ 5 5 6 4 ♮ 6 7 6
39
-stus: ab au- di- ti- o- ne ma- la non ti- me- bit, ab au- di- ti- o- ne
-stus: ab au- di- ti- o- ne ma- la non ti- me- bit, ab au-
- stus. ab au- di- ti- o- ne ma-
-stus: ab au- di- ti- o- ne ma- la non ti- me- bit, ab au- di- ti- o- ne
4 ♯ ♯ 5 ♯ ♮6 5 6 7 6 ♯ 6 6 5 ♯ 5 6

74

57
Et gra- ti- a tu- a il- - lis suc- cur- ren- te, me- re-
Et gra- ti- a tu- a il- lis suc- cur- ren- te, me- re-
Et gra- ti- a tu- a il- lis suc- cur- ren- te, me- re-
Et gra- ti- a tu- a il- lis suc- cur- ren- - te, me- re-
61
-an- tur e- va- de- re ju- di- ci- um ul- ti- o- - nis. Et
-an- tur e- va- de- re ju- di- ci- um ul- ti- o- nis.
-an- tur e- va- de- re ju- di- ci- um ul- ti- o- - nis.
-an- tur e- va- de- re ju- di- ci- um ul- ti- o- nis.
65
lu- cis ae- ter- - - nae be- a- ti-
Et lu- cis ae- ter- nae be- a- ti- tu- di-
Et lu- cis ae- ter- nae be- a- ti- tu- di- ne
be- a- ti- tu- di- ne,

69
-tu- di- ne per- - fru- i, et lu- cis ae- ter-
-ne per- - - fru- i, et lu- cis ae- ter-
per- fru- i, et lu- cis ae- ter- nae, et
et lu- cis ae- ter- nae, et lu- cis ae- ter- -
74
- nae be- a- ti- tu- di- ne, be- a- ti- tu- di- ne
- - nae be- a- ti- tu- di- ne, be- a- ti- tu- di-
lu- cis ae- ter- - nae be- a- ti- tu- di- ne per-
- nae be- a- ti- tu- di- ne, be- a- ti- tu- di-
78
per- - fru- i, per- - - fru- i.
-ne per- - fru- i, per- fru- i.
- - fru- i, per- - - fru- i.
-ne per- - fru- i, per- - - fru- i.

# Sequence

15
ju- dex est ven- tu- rus, Cun- cta stri- cte dis-
- dex est ven- tu- - rus, Cun- - cta stri- - cte, stri- cte dis- cus- su-
ven- tu- rus, Cun- cta stri- cte, stri- cte dis- cus-
20
-cus- su- rus! Tu- ba mi- rum, tu- ba mi- rum spar- - gens so- num
-rus, dis-cus- su- rus! Tu- ba mi- rum spar- - gens so- num Per
-su- rus! Tu- ba mi- rum spar- - gens so- - num
Tu- ba mi- rum, tu- ba mi- rum spar- gens so- num
25
Per se- pul- cra re- gi- o- num, Co- get om- - nes an- - te thro-
se- pul- cra re- gi- o- num, Co- get om- nes an- te thro-
Per se- pul- cra re- gi- o- - num, Co- get om- nes an- te thro-
Per se- pul- cra re- gi- o- num, Co- get om- nes an- te thro-

30
-num. Mors stu- pe- bit et na- tu- ra, Cum re- sur- get cre- a- tu- ra,
-num. Mors stu- pe- bit et na- tu- - ra, Cum re- sur- get cre- a- tu- ra,
-num. Mors stu- pe- bit et na- tu- ra, Cum re- sur- get cre- a- tu- ra,
-num. Mors stu- pe- bit et na- tu- ra, Cum re- sur- get cre- a- tu- ra,
34
Ju- di- can- ti re- spon- su- ra. Li- - ber scri- ptus,
Ju- di- can- ti re- - spon- su- ra. Li- ber scri- ptus, In quo
Ju- di- can- ti re- spon- su- ra. Li- ber scri- ptus pro- fe- re-
Ju- di- can- ti re- spon- su- ra. pro- fe- re- tur,
38
In quo to- tum con- ti- ne- tur, Un- de mun- dus ju- di- ce-
to tum con- ti- ne- - tur, Un- - de mun- dus ju- - di- ce-
-tur, Un- de mun- dus ju- di- ce- tur, ju- di- ce-
con- ti- ne- - tur, Un- de mun- dus ju- di-

42
- tur. Ju- dex er- go cum se- de- - bit,
- tur. Ju- dex er- - go cum se- de- - bit,
- tur. Ju- dex er- go cum se- de- bit,
-ce- tur. Quid- quid
46
Nil in- ul- - tum re- ma-
Quid- quid la- tet, ap- pa- re- bit: Nil in- ul- tum re- ma- ne-
Quid- quid la- tet, ap- - pa- re- bit: Nil in- ul- tum re- ma-
la- tet, ap- pa- re- bit: Nil in- ul- tum re- ma-
49
-ne- bit. Quid sum mi- - ser tunc di- ctu- rus?
- bit. Quid sum mi- ser, quid sum mi- ser tunc di- - ctu- rus?
-ne- bit. Quid sum mi- ser tunc di- ctu- - rus?
-ne- bit. Quid sum mi- - ser tunc di- ctu- rus?

54
Quem pa- tro- num ro- - ga- tu- rus? Cum vix ju- stus sit se- cu-
Quem pa- tro- num ro- ga- tu- rus? Cum vix ju- stus sit
Quem pa- tro- num ro- ga- tu- rus? Cum vix ju- - stus sit se-
Cum vix ju- stus sit se-
58
- rus. Rex tre- men- dae ma- je- sta- tis, Qui sal- van- dos sal- vas gra-
se- cu- rus. Rex tre- men- dae ma- je- sta- - tis, Qui sal- van- dos sal- vas gra-
-cu- rus. Rex tre- men- dae ma- je- sta- tis, Qui sal- van- dos sal- vas gra-
-cu- rus. Rex tre- men- dae ma- je- sta- tis,
62
-tis, Sal- va me, fons pi- e- ta- - tis. Re- - cor- da- re
-tis, Sal- va me, sal- va me, fons pi- e- ta- - tis. Re- cor- da-
-tis, Sal- - va me, sal- va me, fons pi- e- ta- tis. Re- cor- da-
Sal- va me, sal- va me, fons pi- e- ta- tis.

67
Je- su pi- - e, Quod sum cau- sa tu- - ae vi-
-re Je- su pi- e, Quod sum cau- sa tu- ae vi-
-re Je- su pi- e, Quod sum cau- sa tu- ae vi-
71
-ae: Ne me per- - das, ne me per- das il- la di- e.
- ae: Ne me per- das ne me per- das il- - la di- e.
-ae: Ne me per- - das, ne me per- das il- la di- e.
Quae-
75
Quae- rens me, se- di- sti las- - sus: Re- de- mi- sti
Quae- rens me, se- di- sti las- sus: Re- de-
Quae- - rens me, se- di- sti las- - sus: Re- de-
- rens me, se- di- sti las- - sus: Re- de-

80
cru- cem pas- - sus: Tan- - tus la- bor non sit cas-
-mi- sti cru- cem pas- sus: Tan- tus la- bor
-mi- sti cru- cem pas- sus: Tan- tus la- bor non
-mi- sti cru- cem pas- sus: Tan- tus la- bor non sit
84
- sus. Ju- - ste ju- dex ul- ti- o-
non sit cas- sus. Ju- ste ju- dex ul- ti- o- nis, ul- ti- o-
sit cas- sus. Ju- ste ju- dex ul- ti- o-
cas- sus. Ju- ste ju- dex ul- ti- o-
89
- nis, Do- num fac re- mis- si- o- - nis, An- te di- em ra- ti- o-
-nis, Do- num fac re- mis- si- o- nis, An- te di- em ra- ti- o-
-nis, Do- - num fac re- mis- si- o- nis, An- te di- em ra- ti- o-
-nis, An- te di- em ra- ti- o-

84

108
la- tro- nem ex- - au- di- sti, Mi- - hi quo- que
Et la- tro- nem ex- au- di- sti, Mi- - hi quo-
-au- di- sti, Mi- hi quo- que spem de- di- sti,
-tro- nem ex- au- di- sti, ex- au- di- sti, Mi- hi quo- que
112
spem de- di- sti. Sed tu bo-
-que spem de- di- sti. Pre- ces me- ae non sunt di- - gnae:
de- di- sti. Pre- ces me- ae non sunt di- gnae:
spem de- di- sti. Sed tu bo-
116
- nus fac be- ni- - gne, Ne pe- ren- - ni cre- mer i-
Sed tu bo- nus fac be- ni- - gne, Ne pe- ren- - ni cre- mer i-
Sed tu bo- - nus fac be- ni- gne, Ne pe- ren- ni cre- mer
- nus fac be- ni- gne.

120
- gne. In- ter o- ves lo- - cum prae- sta, Sta-
- gne. In- ter o- ves lo- cum prae- sta, Et ab hae- dis me se-
i- gne. In- ter o- ves lo- cum prae- sta, Et ab hae- dis me se-
In- ter o- ves lo- cum prae- sta, Et ab hae- dis me se-
124
- tu- ens in par- te, in par- te de- - xtra. Con- fu- ta- tis ma- le- di- ctis,
-que- stra, Sta- tu- ens in par- te de- xtra. Con- fu-
-que- stra, Sta- - tu- ens in par- te de- xtra. Con- fu- ta- tis ma-
-que- stra, Sta- tu- ens in par- te de- xtra. Con- fu- ta-
128
ma- le- di- ctis, Flam- mis a- cri- bus ad- di- ctis, Vo- ca me cum be- ne- di-
-ta- tis ma- le- di- ctis, Flam- mis a- cri- bus ad- di- ctis, Vo- - ca me cum
- le- di- ctis, Vo- - ca me cum be- ne- di- ctis, cum
-tis ma- le- di- ctis, Flam- mis a- cri- bus ad- di- ctis, Vo- ca me cum be- ne- di-

132
- ctis. O- ro sup- - plex et ac- cli- nis,
be- ne- di- ctis. O- - ro sup- plex et ac- cli- nis, et ac- cli-
be- ne- di- ctis. O- ro sup- plex, Cor con-
-ctis. O- ro sup- plex et ac- cli- nis,
136
Cor con- tri- tum qua- si ci- nis: Ge re cu-
-nis, et ac- cli- nis: Ge- re cu- ram me- i fi- nis,
-tri- tum qua- si ci- nis: Ge- re cu- ram me- i,
Cor con- tri- tum qua- si ci- nis:
140
-ram me- i fi- - nis.
me i fi - nis.
me- i fi- nis, me- i fi- - - nis.
Ge- re cu- ram me- i fi- nis.

144
Adagio
La- cri- mo- - sa, la- cri- mo- -
La- cri- mo- sa, la- cri- - mo- -
La- cri- mo- sa, la- cri- mo- -
La- cri- mo- sa, la- cri- mo- -
149
- - sa di- es il- - la, Qua re- sur-
- sa di- es il- la, Qua re- sur- - get ex fa- vil-
- - sa di- es il- la, Qua re- sur- get ex fa-
- sa di- es il- la, Qua re- sur- get
154
- get ex fa- vil- la, ex fa- vil- - la Ju- di- can- dus ho- mo re-
-la, qua re- sur- - get ex fa- vil- la Ju- di- can- dus ho- mo re-
-vil- la, re- sur- get ex fa- vil- la Ju- di- can- dus ho- mo re-
ex fa- vil- la Ju- di- can- dus ho- mo re-

158
-us: Hu- ic er- go par- ce De- us.
-us: Hu- ic er- - go par- ce De- - us. Do-
-us: Hu- ic er- go par- ce De- - us.
-us: Hu- ic er- go par- - ce De- us. Pi- e Je- su
163
Pi- e Je- su Do- mi- ne, do- na e- is
- na e- is re- qui- em, pi- e Je- su Do- mi- ne, do-
Do- na e- is re- - - qui- em,
Do- mi- ne, do- - na e- is re- - qui- em,
167
re- - - qui- em, do-
- na e- is re- - qui- em, do- na e- is re- qui- em,
do- na e- is re- qui- em, do- na e- is
pi- e Je- su Do- mi- ne, do- - na e- is re- qui-

171
- na e- is re- - qui- em, pi- - e Je- su Do-
pi- e Je- su Do- mi- ne, do- na e- is re-
re- - - qui- em, pi- e Je- su
-em, do- na e- is re- qui- em,
175
- mi- ne, do- - na e- is re- qui- em, do- na e-
- - - qui- em. A-
Do- mi- ne, do- - na e- is re- qui- em, do- - na e- is re- qui-
pi- e Je- su Do- mi- ne, do- na e- is re- qui- em.
179
- is re- qui- em. A- - men, a- - - men.
- - men, a- men.
-em. A- - men, a- men.
A- - men, a- men.

## Offertory

15
-de- li- um de- fun- cto- - - rum, om-
- ni- um fi- de- li- um de- fun- cto- rum, li- be- ra a- ni- mas om- ni- um fi-
- rum, li- be- ra a- ni- mas om- - ni- um fi- de- li-
li- - be- ra a- ni- mas om- ni- um fi- de- li- um
19
- ni- um fi- de- li- um de- fun- - cto- rum de poe- -
-de- li- um de- - fun- cto- - rum de poe- -
-um de- fun- cto- - rum de poe- nis
de- fun- cto- - rum de poe-
24
- nis in- fer- ni, et de pro- fun- do la-
-nis in- - fer- ni, et de pro- fun- do la-
in- fer- - ni, et de pro- fun- do la-
-nis in- fer- ni, et de pro- fun- do la-

29
-cu: li- be- ra e- as de o- re le- o- nis, ne ab- sor-
-cu: li- be- ra e- as de o- re le- o- nis,
- cu: li- be- ra e- as de o- re le- o- nis, ne ab-
-cu: li- be- ra e- as de o- re le- o- nis, ne
34
- be- at e- as tar- ta- rus, ne ab- sor- be- at e- - as, ne
ne ab- sor- be- at e- as tar- ta- rus, ne ab- sor- be- at e- as tar- ta-
-sor- be- at e- as tar- ta- rus, ne ab- sor- - be- at e- as tar- ta-
ab- sor- be- at e- as tar- ta- rus, ne ab- sor- be- at e- as tar- ta-
39
ca- - dant, ne ca- - dant in ob- scu- rum:
-rus, ne ca- - dant, ne ca- - dant in ob- scu- rum:
-rus, ne ca- - dant in ob- scu- - rum:
-rus, ne ca- - dant in ob- scu- - rum:

44
sed si- gni- fer san- ctus Mi- cha- el re- prae- sen- tet e- as,
sed si- gni- fer san- ctus Mi- cha- el re- prae- sen- tet
sed si- gni- fer san- ctus Mi- cha- el re- prae-
48
re-prae- sen- tet e- as in lu- cem, in lu- cem san- ctam:
e- as, re- prae- sen- tet e- as in lu- cem san- ctam:
-sen- tet, re- prae- sen- tet e- as in lu- cem, in lu- cem san- ctam:
in lu- cem, in lu- cem san- ctam:
54
Quam o- lim A- bra- hae pro- mi- si- sti, et se- mi- ni
Quam o- lim A- bra- hae pro- mi- si- sti,
Quam o- lim A- bra- hae pro- mi-
Quam o- lim A- bra- hae

59
e- - jus, quam o- lim A- bra-
et se- mi- ni e- - jus, quam o- lim
-si- sti, et se- mi- ni e- - -
pro- mi- si- sti, et se- mi- ni e- jus,
64
-hae pro- mi- si- sti, quam o- lim A- bra- hae, quam o- lim
A- bra-hae pro- mi- si- - sti, quam o- lim A- bra-hae
-jus, quam o- lim A- bra- hae pro- - mi- si-
quam o- lim A- bra- hae pro- mi- si- sti,
69
A- bra- hae pro- - mi- si- - sti, et
et se- mi- ni e- - jus,
-sti, et se- mi- ni e- -
et se- mi- ni e- jus, et se- mi- ni e-

[Fine]

97

101
-mus, me- mo- ri- am fa- ci- mus: fac e- as, Do- mi- ne,
- - ci- mus: fac e- as, Do- mi- ne, fac e-
-mus, fa- - ci- mus: fac e- as, Do- mi- ne, fac
me- mo- ri- am fa- ci- mus: fac
106
de mor- - te trans- i- re ad vi- - -
-as, Do- mi- ne, de mor- te trans- i- - re ad vi-
e- as, Do- mi- ne, de mor- te trans- i- re ad vi- -
e- as, Do- mi- ne de mor- te trans- i- - re ad vi-
112
-tam, de mor- - te, trans- i- re ad vi-
-tam, de mor- te, de mor- te trans- i- re ad vi- -
-tam, de mor- - te trans- i- re ad vi-
-tam, de mor- te, de mor- te trans- i- - re ad

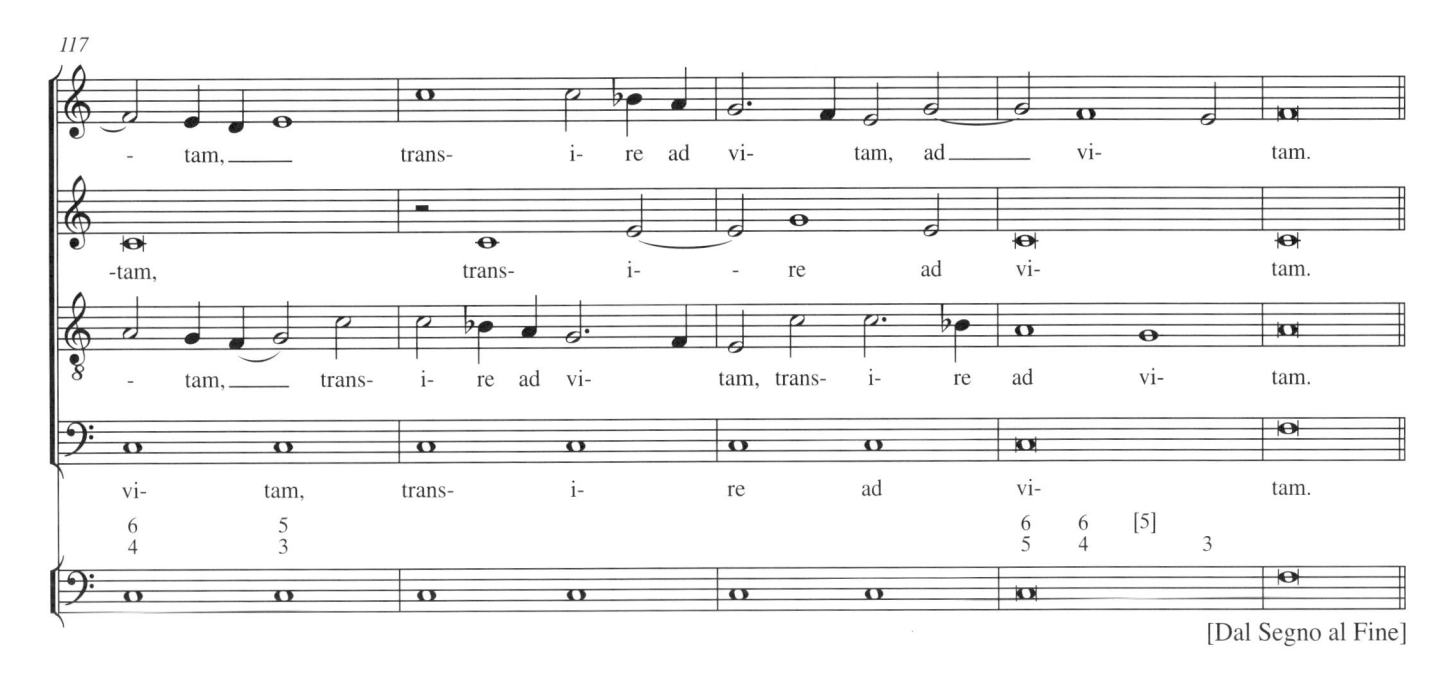

## Sanctus

11
- - ctus, San- - -
- ctus, San- - - -
San- - - ctus, San- -
- - ctus, San- - -
16
-ctus Do- mi- nus De- us Sa- ba- oth.
-ctus Do- mi- nus De- us Sa- ba- oth.
- ctus Do- mi- nus De- us Sa- ba- oth.
-ctus Do- mi- nus De- us Sa- ba- oth.
21
Ple- ni sunt cae- li et ter- ra glo- ri- a tu- a.
Ple- ni sunt cae- li et ter- ra glo- ri- a tu- a.
Ple- ni sunt cae- li et ter- ra glo- ri- a tu- a.
Ple- ni sunt cae- li et ter- ra glo- ri- a tu- a.

27
Ho- san- na in ex- cel- - sis,
Ho- san- na in ex- cel- - - - sis,
Ho- san- na in ex- cel- - sis, Ho-
Ho- san- na in ex- cel-
32
Ho- - san- na in ex- cel-
Ho- san- na in ex- cel- sis, in
-san- na in ex- cel- - - - sis,
- - - sis, Ho- san-
37
- - sis, Ho- san- na
ex- cel- - - - sis, Ho-
Ho- san- na in ex- cel- - sis,
-na in ex- cel- sis, Ho- san- na in ex- cel- -

in ex- cel- - sis.
-san- na in ex- cel- - sis, in ex- cel- - sis.
in ex- cel- - sis, in ex- cel- sis.
- sis, in ex- cel- sis.

[Fine]

Be- ne- di- ctus qui ve- nit, qui ve- nit, be- ne-
Be- ne- di- ctus qui ve- - - nit,
Be- ne- di- ctus qui ve- - - nit,

-di- ctus qui ve- nit in no- mi- ne Do- - mi-
be- ne- di- ctus qui ve- nit in no- mi- ne Do- mi-
be- ne- di- ctus qui ve- nit in no- mi- ne Do- - mi-

## Agnus Dei

-i, qui tol- lis pec- ca- ta mun- - di, mun-
- gnus De- i, qui tol- lis pec- ca- ta mun-
-lis pec- ca- - ta mun- di, pec- ca- ta,
qui tol- lis, qui tol- lis pec- ca- ta
- di, A- - gnus De- i,
- di, A- - gnus
A- gnus De- i, qui tol- lis pec- ca-
mun- di, A- gnus De- i, qui tol- lis pec-
qui tol- lis pec- ca- ta, pec- ca- ta mun- - di:
De- i, qui tol- lis pec- ca- ta mun- di:
- ta mun- - di, qui tol- lis pec- ca- ta mun- di:
-ca- ta, qui tol- lis pec- ca- - ta mun- di:

do- na e- is re- qui- em, re- - qui-
do- na e- is re- qui- em, do- na e- is re- qui-
do- na e- is re- - - qui-
do- na e- is, do- na e- is re- - qui-
-em. A- - gnus De- - - i, qui tol- lis pec-
-em. A- - - gnus De- - i, qui
-em. A- - gnus De- - i, qui tol-
-em. A- - gnus De- i, qui tol-
-ca- ta mun- - - di: do- na e- is, do- na e-
tol- lis pec- ca- ta mun- - di. do- na e- is
-lis pec- ca- ta mun- - di: do- na e- - is, do- na
-lis pec- ca- ta mun- - di: do- na e-

35
-is, do- -na e- is re- -qui- em. A-
re- qui- em, re- -qui- em. A-
e- is, do- na e- is re- qui- em. A-
- is re- - qui- em.
39
-gnus De- i, A- gnus De-
-gnus De- - - i, A- - gnus De-
-gnus De- - - i, qui tol-
A- - gnus De- -
44
-i, qui tol- lis pec- ca- ta mun-
-i, qui tol- - lis pec- ca- ta mun-
- lis pec- ca- ta mun- di, qui tol- - lis pec- ca- ta
-i, qui tol- - lis pec- ca- ta mun- di,

49
- di, pec- ca- ta mun- di: do- na e-
-di, qui tol- - lis pec- ca- ta mun- di: do- - na e-
mun- di, qui tol- lis pec- ca- ta mun- - di: do- na e-
qui tol- lis pec- ca- - ta mun- di: do- na e-
54
-is re- qui- em sem- pi- ter- nam, do- na e- is re- qui-
-is re- qui- em sem- pi- ter- nam, do- na e- is re-
-is re- qui- em sem- pi- ter- nam, do- na e- is re-
-is re- qui- em sem- pi- ter- nam, do- na e- is re- qui-
59
-em sem- pi- ter- - - nam.
- qui- em sem- pi- ter- - nam.
- qui- em sem- - pi- ter- - - nam
-em sem- pi- ter- - - nam.

# Communion

16
tu- is in ae- ter- - num, qui- a pi-
-ter- - - num, cum san- ctis tu-
-is in ae- ter- - - num, cum san- ctis
Cum san- ctis tu- is in ae-
21
-us es, cum san- ctis tu- is in ae- ter-
-is in ae- ter- - num, qui-
tu- is in ae- ter- - num, cum san- ctis tu- is in
-ter- - num, qui- a pi- us
25
- - - -
-a pi- us es, cum
ae- ter- - num, qui-
es, cum san- ctis tu- is in ae- ter-

29
-num, in ae- ter- - - num, cum san- ctis tu-
san- ctis tu- is in ae- ter- - num, qui-
- a pi- us es, cum san- ctis tu- is in ae-
-num, qui- a pi- us es,
5 6 ♭6 6 5 6 ♭ ♭
34
-is in ae- ter- - - num, cum san- ctis
-a pi- us es, cum san- ctis tu-
-ter- - num, in ae- ter- - num,
cum san- ctis tu- is in ae- ter- -
5 6 6 5 ♭ 6
38
tu- is in ae- ter- - - num, qui- a pi- us
-is in ae- ter- - num, qui- a pi- us es, pi- us
cum san- ctis tu- is in ae- ter- - num, qui- - a pi- us
-num, qui- a pi- us es, qui- a pi- us
6 ♭ ♯ [♯] ♭ 4 ♯ ♭

43
es. Re- qui- em ae- ter- nam, ae- ter- - nam
es. Re- qui- em ae- ter- - nam
es. Re- qui- em ae- ter- - nam
es. Re- qui- em ae- ter- nam
[Fine]
48
do- na e- is Do- - mi- ne: et lux per-
do- na e- is Do- - mi- ne: et lux per-
do- na e- is Do- - mi- ne: et lux
do- na e- is Do- - mi- ne: et
53
-pe- tu- a lu- ce- at e- - - is.
-pe- tu- a lu- ce- at e- - - - is. Cum
per pe- tu- a lu- ce- at e- - - is.
lux per- pe- tu- a lu- ce- at e- - - is.
[Dal Segno al Fine]

# Critical Report

## Sources

### Salve Regina

The primary source for this edition is the autograph score, University of Cambridge, Fitzwilliam Museum, Mu. Ms. 225, fols. 9r–12v. The composition is not titled, but folio 9r is dated "Febraro 1703." (upper left) and signed "D'Alessandro Scarlatti" (upper right). Mu. Ms. 225 also contains the part of the Fanciullo from the oratorio *La Jezabel* of Pietro Paolo Bencini on folios 1r–8v and the autograph score of Scarlatti's cantata *Sciolta da freddi amplessi,* dated "1 maggio 1704," on folios 13r–15r.

The volume belongs to the Aylesford Collection, one of the most important for research on Handel, which was collected by Handel's friend and librettist Charles Jennens. He was also a friend of Edward Holdsworth, who in 1742 succeeded in buying for Jennens a substantial part of the library of Cardinal Pietro Ottoboni, including autographs of Scarlatti, Vivaldi, Albinoni, Pietro Paolo Bencini, Carlo Francesco Cesarini, Francesco Mancini, Benedetto Marcello, Carlo Francesco Pollarolo, Domenico Natale Sarro, and others.[1] In 1918 Edward Dent purchased the manuscript from the estate of Jennens's descendent, the earl of Aylesford, and consigned it in 1941 to the Fitzwilliam Museum.[2]

Two further sources mentioned in the literature on Scarlatti, one in the Österreichische Nationalbibliothek and one in a private collection in London, are now lost.[3]

### Miserere

The primary source for this edition are the manuscript choirbooks, Biblioteca Apostolica Vaticana, Cappella Sistina 188–89. The title page for Cappella Sistina 188 reads: "Miserere | Primus Chorus | Nouem Vocibus | D.[ominus] Alex. Scarlatti | Thomas Altavilla Scribebat an[n]o 1711." The title page for Cappella Sistina 189 reads: "Miserere | Secundus Chorus | Nouem Vocibus | D.[ominus] Alex. Scarlatti | Thomas Altavilla Scribebat anno D[omi]ni 1711." Altavilla was active as a copyist in the Sistine Chapel from 1701 to 1715.

### Magnificat

The primary source for this edition is the manuscript score, Münster, Diözesanbibliothek, Santini-Sammlung, Sant. Hs. 3874, copied by Santini in 1835. The title page (fol. 1) reads: "1744 | Magnificat | a Cinque | del Cavaliere Alessandro Scarlatti | Estratto [?] dal suo Originale presso il Maestro Terziani 1835."[4] On folio 1v appears "Magnificat a 5 P[ri]mi toni."

Another source is Regensburg, Bischöfliche Zentralbibliothek, Proske-Musikbibliothek, Scarlatti I/5. According to Benedikt Poensgen this manuscript was copied by Carl Proske.[5]

### Missa defunctorum

The primary source for this edition is the partially autograph score, Bergamo, Biblioteca Donizetti, fondo Piatti-Lochis 9262. The score consists of twenty-nine folios. The first page of music (fol. 1) has at the left the autograph indication: "Missa | Defunctorum | Quatuor Vocibus | C.A.T.B. | 1717. | Originale." Other indications on the title page are in various other hands: "John Stanley M.B." (beside the title), "à battuta giusta" (the tempo indication), "Del Sig[no]r Caval[ier]e Aless.[and]ro Scarlatti" (at the right just above the music), and "Ro" (partially erased) and "Ros[?]" (at the upper left and right corners, respectively). The large ornamented initial *R*'s are autograph and very similar to those of the *Salve Regina* in Mu. Ms. 225 (see above). According to the catalogue of Rostirolla, the manuscript is entirely autograph.[6] However, the only section that is definitively autograph is the Sequence, while the rest was prepared by a copyist, who according to Ute Schacht-Pape could be either Domenico Castrucci or Tarquinio Lanciani.[7] The attribution to the latter seems rather dubious when compared to another sample of music by this copyist.[8] Scarlatti probably wrote the Sequence during or immediately after the copying of the first part of the *Missa defunctorum* since the type of paper used is the same. The succeeding sections were written by the same copyist but on different paper. In any case, the entire manuscript was certainly realized under the guidance of the composer, as attested by his numerous autograph annotations.

The name "John Stanley M.B.," overlooked by Schacht-Pape, is very important, testifying that the manuscript arrived in England during the eighteenth century and belonged to the organist and composer John Stanley (London, 1712–86). The letters "M.B." celebrate the fact that Stanley, in 1729, was the youngest to obtain the degree of bachelor of music at Oxford University. He used these letters also on the title pages of editions of his own music.[9] The fact that this manuscript arrived in

England around the middle of the eighteenth century suggests that it was part of the above-mentioned group of Italian manuscripts acquired by English agents. Stanley was a collector, and his library was sold in the year of his death by the auction house Christie's in London.[10] The manuscript probably remained in England. According to Schacht-Pape it was in the possession of C. E. Horsley, who in 1858 helped found the Library of the Musical Society of London,[11] and it passed subsequently to Alfredo Piatti (b. Bergamo, 1822; d. Crocetto di Mozzo, 1901). Piatti, a teacher and concert artist active throughout Europe who was considered one of the major violoncellists of the nineteenth century, settled definitively in London in 1846 and remained there for almost fifty years. The fondo Piatti-Lochis consists of 1,289 volumes that made up Piatti's personal library, integrated with volumes added by his daughter, Countess Rosa Piatti-Lochis.

Other manuscripts (all of them copyists' scores from the nineteenth century) and editions of the *Missa defunctorum* include:

1. Münster, Diözesanbibliothek, Santini-Sammlung, Sant. Hs. 3872, ca. 1820.
2. Ibid., Santini-Sammlung, Sant. Hs. 3873, ca. 1820.
3. Munich, Theatinerkirche St. Kajetan, Mk 779, ca. 1840.[12]
4. Berlin, Staatsbibliothek Preußischer Kulturbesitz, Mus. Ms. 19624.
5. Munich, St. Michael Mm 955/1.[13]
6. Munich, Bayerische Staatsbibliothek, Mus. Ms. 1033; before 1840.
7. Ibid., Cod. lat. 1512; nineteenth century, containing only the *Benedictus*.
8. Paris, Bibliothèque Nationale, D. 11893, ca. 1820.
9. *Missa pro defunctis a 4 voci e organo*, ed. Alexandre Choron, Journal de chant et musique d'eglise (Paris: Ruault, 1830), 22–28.
10. *Missa pro defunctis: für vier Stimmen mit nich obligater Orgelbegleitung von A. Scarlatti* (Leipzig: Braun, 1884).
11. *Missa pro defunctis 4 v.*, ed. S. Lück, Oeuvres choisies des meilleurs compositeurs de musique religieuse classique, vol. 5 (Leipzig: Braun, 1884/85).
12. *Missa "Pro defunctis": a 4 voci miste / Alessandro Scarlatti*, ed. Mario Fabbri (Arezzo: Associazione degli amici della musica di Arezzo, [1984?]), not for sale.

The copies in Münster were made by Fortunato Santini and are not derived from the manuscript in Bergamo, because they lack the Sequence. They served as the model for all manuscripts and editions in the nineteenth century.[14]

## Editorial Methods

Original indications of the vocal parts have been preserved, and added in brackets when lacking. Original C clefs for the voices have been changed to treble and transposing treble clefs per modern practice. Cleffing in the basso continuo parts has been standardized to G2 or F4 clefs as appropriate. Original time signatures and key signatures have been preserved throughout, with the exception of the "Deposuit potentes" section in the *Magnificat*, where the original C has been transcribed as ¢. Editorial additions to the scores are indicated as follows: slurs and ties are dashed, cautionary accidentals are placed in parentheses, and other additions are placed in brackets.

Original note values are maintained, except that tied notes within a measure are altered to the total note value where appropriate (e.g., two tied half notes are altered to one whole note, or a half tied to a quarter altered to a dotted half). Beaming has been standardized according to modern practice. Slurs are extended to enclose ties according to modern practice. Original barring is retained even where the time signature is contradicted, as in the following cases: the *Salve Regina* (mm. 59, 126); the *Magnificat* (mm. 46, 111, 161, 289, 291); and the *Missa defunctorum* (Introit, m. 11; Sequence, mm. 108, 168; Offertory, mm. 9, 30, 53, 55, 63, 99; Sanctus, mm. 32, 50; Agnus Dei, mm.10, 11, 37, 45; and Communion, m. 24). In the *Miserere* all barring is editorial, and certain passages are barred so as to begin with incomplete measures (mm. 15, 31, 74, 114, 133). Some other modifications of barring are mentioned in the critical notes. All repeat indications have been realized or modernized.

Bass figures in the edition are placed above the staff; in the sources they are written both above and below the staff. Obsolete forms, such as the use of ♯ for ♮, have been modernized without comment. Where the scale degree 3 is inflected by an accidental, as in "♯3," the numeral is tacitly removed to leave only the accidental; this is also true in cases where the inflection (usually ♮) reinforces the key signature. A raised third has been tacitly assumed in the context of cadential 4–3 suspensions. Minor adjustments in the placement of continuo figures have been made tacitly when supported by the musical context. Figures that are incorrect in the source have been removed or corrected and are reported in the critical notes.

Accidentals in the edition are valid through the end of the measure. Accidentals redundant according to this modern rule have been tacitly deleted. In cases where an editorial accidental precedes the first inflection of the same pitch in the source, both accidentals are given in the edition. As with the figured bass, the modern use of the natural sign has been adopted.

The spelling of the texts has been modernized. The punctuation and syllabification also follow modern conventions, and the customary "ij" and "&" signs have been replaced tacitly by the relevant text. Other additions to the text are given in angle brackets. In the *Missa defunctorum*, the organ part includes incipits for each section ("Requiem," etc.), which are omitted from the edition. As with other *Miserere* settings for the Sistine Chapel between the sixteenth and seventeenth centuries, Scarlatti did not set the even-numbered verses of the *Miserere*, which were performed from memory.[15] For these the plainchant has been added using psalm tone 2 transposed up a fourth, according to common seventeenth-century practice.[16]

# Critical Notes

The following abbreviations are used in these critical notes: C = Cantus, A = Altus, T = Tenor, B = Bassus, Org. = Organ (continuo), sbr = semibreve. Notes are numbered consecutively within a measure. Where appropriate, beats are counted rather than notes. Pitches are identified using the system in which c' = middle C.

## *Miserere*

Primus Chorus, over initial, each part is marked "Paulatim" (in alternation). M. 148, all voices, "Omnes" is marked above each staff.

## *Magnificat*

M. 23, Org., figure $^{\sharp 4}_{2}$ is on note 1. M. 29, T, note 7 has $\sharp$. M. 35, C2, beat 1, note 1 is missing. M. 39, Org., note 2 is e. M. 40, C2, notes 1 and 2 are half–half. M. 50, Org., notes 2–3 are a–f. M. 62, Org., note 2 has figure $\flat$. M. 95, Org., note 3, figure is 6. M. 117, Org., note 7 has figure $^{7}_{6}$. M. 122, A, note 1 is not clearly legible. M. 136, Org., note 2 is d. M. 144, Org., note 3 has figure 6–7. M. 146, time signature is ¢. Mm. 146–60, C1, C2, A, T, B, text is "deposuis" throughout with the exception of m. 151, A, T. M. 168, T, note 5 is d'. M. 195, Org., note 6 has $\sharp$. M. 199, Org., note 6 has figure 6–7. M. 209, Org., note 1 is half. M. 229, C2, text is "-ae." M. 274, A, notes 3–6 are e'–f'–g'–a' (pitches supplied from m. 272). M. 276, Org. is marked "Gloria Patri." M. 285, Org. is marked "a 3"; note 2 has figure 5–6. M. 286, Org., beat 4 is marked "a 5." Mm. 292–413, Org., all pitches and figures are editorial except m. 308, note 2, and m. 309, note 1. M. 303, C1, note 2 is c". M. 309, Org., note 1 is whole. M. 316, T, note 9 is c$\sharp$' 8th. M. 350, A, note 5 is c'. M. 381, C2, note 1 is missing.

## *Missa defunctorum*

### INTROIT

M. 3, Org., note 1 has figure $^{9}_{8}$. M. 5 Org., beginning of bar has an asterisk; C, A, T, B have a design of a hand with the index finger indicating the staff. M. 20, C, notes 3–5 are dotted quarter–8th–half; note 5 is tied to note 1 of m. 21. M. 25, Org., note 1 has figure $^{4}_{\sharp 3}$. M. 45, intervening barline appears after beat 1 of m. 45. M. 45, Org., note 3 has figure 7–6. M. 46, Org., note 2 has figure 5–6 above and figure 7–6 below. M. 59, Org., note 3 has figure $\flat$ above and figure 6–5 below. After the double barline at m. 81 each staff is marked "Requiem da capo."

### KYRIE

M. 7, C, notes 1–2, source shows handwritten alteration of rhythm from dotted half–quarter to dotted quarter–8th. M. 23 is divided into two measures. M. 24, Org., note 4 has figure 5–6. M. 34, Org., note 2 has figures $^{7}_{\sharp}$ $^{6}_{4-3}$.

### GRADUAL

Over opening staff, title "Graduale." M. 3, C has b♭' half–g' half–b♭' whole. M. 5, C, A, T, B are marked "dona come sopra da capo" (autograph); A, T, B, have a design of a hand with the index finger indicating the staff; Org. is marked with an asterisk and "come sopra da capo infino: luceat | eis, e poi come qui siegue" (autograph). M. 32, C, notes 3–4 are corrected to dotted quarter–8th in another hand. M. 41, C, notes 4 and 5, the syllables "ti-me" are erased. M. 51 is divided into two bars. M. 53 is divided into two bars. M. 61 is divided into two bars. M. 64 is divided into two bars. M. 77, B.c., figure 6 is on note 2. M. 81, Org., note 1 has figure 2. After final barline, "siegue subb.[it]o la sequentia: Dies irae &c." (autograph).

### SEQUENCE

At top of page: "Sequentia Dies ire [sic] attacca subb.[it]o | Si canta a battuta moderata, di due tempi sì, mà non stretta." (autograph). M. 9, Org. is marked "T." above, "a 3." below staff (autograph). M. 21, Org., staff under note 2 is marked "a 4." M. 74, C, note 3 is a'. M. 144, A, text is "lagrimosa." M. 145, Org., note 1 has figure $\sharp 6$ below and figure 4–0 above. M. 149, Org., note 1 has figure 5–6 below and figure 7–6 above. M. 182, the final double bar is crossed out.

### OFFERTORY

Top of page is marked "Offertorium." M. 1, C, notes 1–3 altered in another hand from dotted whole–half–half. M. 2, C, note 2 altered in another hand from whole. M. 39, T, note 1 is b♭. M. 40, Org., note 3 has figure ♮. M. 54, the left margin of each staff has repeat ritornello sign. M. 73, Org., note 2 has figure 5. M. 79, Org. is marked "Hostias." M. 82 is divided into two bars. M. 91, note 3, and m. 92, notes 1–3, C has text "-dis offe-" crossed out and rewritten above staff. M. 92 is divided into two bars; A, note 4 has text crossed out. Mm. 92–93, usual text "tu suscipe" does not appear in this source. M. 107 is divided into two bars. M. 119 is divided into two bars. At the end of Offertorio on the C staff is marked "Come sopra" (autograph) and the incipit of "Quam olim" (the first three notes); on the A staff "Come sopra" and the incipit of "Quam olim" (the first note); on B and Org. staff "Come sopra" (autograph); at the right of the staff there is a design of a hand with the index finger indicating the da capo sign.

### SANCTUS

M. 2, C, Org., the parallel fifths have been marked with two X's. M. 12, Org., note 3 has figure 7–6. M. 20, at the end of each staff there is a double barline crossed out. M. 63, after final barline, C, B, Org. are marked "Osanna"; A, T have first two notes of "Osanna" with text.

### AGNUS DEI

M. 53, T, note 1 is f'. M. 35 is divided into two bars. M. 54 is divided into two bars.

### COMMUNION

M. 15 is divided into two bars. M. 46, C has b♭' half–g' half–b♭' whole. M. 47, Org., second figure is $^{\flat 5}_{3}$. M. 57, A, note 2 is sbr. At the end, C, A, T, B, Org.: "Cum sanctis al segno ※"; on the right: "L. D. B. V."

# Notes

1. John H. Roberts, "The Aylesford Collection," in *Handel Collections and Their History*, ed. Terence Best, 39–85 (Oxford: Clarendon Press, 1993), 44.

2. Benedikt Johannes Poensgen, "Die Offiziumskompositionen von Alessandro Scarlatti" (Ph.D. diss., University of Hamburg, 2004), 1:60.

3. Ibid., 2:49.

4. Pietro Terziani (1765–1831) was a Roman composer who produced a large repertoire of sacred music.

5. Poensgen, "Offiziumskompositionen," 2:30. There is also a modern edition: Alessandro Scarlatti, *Vespro della Beata Vergine*, ed. Jörg Jacobi (Bremen: Edition baroque, 2006), 84–125.

6. Giancarlo Rostirolla, "Catalogo generale delle opere," in *Alessandro Scarlatti*, by Roberto Pagano, Giancarlo Rostirolla, and Lino Bianchi (Turin: ERI, 1972), 513.

7. Ute Schacht-Pape, *Das Messenschaffen von Alessandro Scarlatti* (Frankfurt am Main: Peter Lang, 1993), 33.

8. Ibid., 106 n. 3; Ursula Kirkendale, *Antonio Caldara: Life and Venetian-Roman Oratorios* (Florence: Olschki, 2007), plate 17.

9. See *The New Grove Dictionary of Music and Musicians*, 2nd ed., s.v. "Stanley, John" (pp. 287–89), by Malcolm Boyd and Glyn Williams. In a 1775 collection of his concertos published in London, the frontispiece reads: *Six Concertos | for the Organ, Harpsichord, or | Forte Piano; | With Accompanyment | for two Violins and a Bass, | Composed by | JOHN STANLEY, M.B. | Organist*. Quoted in John Wilson, "John Stanley: Some Opus Numbers and Editions," *Music and Letters* 39, no. 4 (1958): 359.

10. Alec Hyatt King, *Some British Collectors of Music, c. 1600–1960* (Cambridge: Cambridge University Press, 1963), 20, 132.

11. Schacht-Pape, *Messenschaffen*, 33–34.

12. Siegfried Gmeinwieser, *Die Musikhandschriften in der Theatinerkirche St. Kajetan in München: Thematischer Katalog* (Munich: G. Henle, 1979), 119.

13. Hildegard Herrmann-Schneider, *Die Musikhandschriften der St. Michaelskirche in München: Thematischer Katalog* (Munich: G. Henle, 1985), 228.

14. Schacht-Pape, *Messenschaffen*, 34–35.

15. See the *Miserere* anthology in Biblioteca Apostolica Vaticana, Cappella Sistina 205–6, which contains settings by Palestrina, Gregorio Allegri, Fabrizio Dentice, Felice and Francesco Anerio, Domenico Nanino, and Ruggero Giovanelli. See also the *Miserere* of Matteo Simonelli, Biblioteca Apostolica Vaticana, Cappella Sistina, 192; and the *Miserere* of Tommaso Bai, copied in 1713, Cappella Sistina, 203–4.

16. The psalm tone chosen can be found in Adriano Banchieri, *Cartella musicale* (Venice, 1614), 70–71, cited in *The New Grove Dictionary of Music and Musicians*, 2nd ed., s.v. "Mode" (p. 817), by Harold S. Powers and Frans Wiering. Numerous treatises describe the use of transposed psalm tones (or *tuoni ecclesiastici*) as a basis for polyphonic composition, with the transposed second tone consistently associated with a G final and one flat in the key signature. For more, see Gregory Barnett, "Tonal Organization in Seventeenth-Century Music Theory," in *Cambridge History of Western Music Theory*, ed. Thomas Christensen, 407–55 (Cambridge: Cambridge University Press, 2002); Harold S. Powers, "From Psalmody to Tonality," in *Tonal Structures in Early Music*, ed. Cristle Collins Judd, 341–72 (New York: Garland, 1998); and Michael Dodds, "The Baroque Church Tones in Theory and Practice" (Ph.D. diss., Eastman School of Music of the University of Rochester, 1999).

Recent Researches in the Music of the Baroque Era
Steven Saunders, general editor

| Vol. | Composer: Title |
| --- | --- |
| 1 | Marc-Antoine Charpentier: *Judicium Salomonis* |
| 2 | Georg Philipp Telemann: *Forty-eight Chorale Preludes* |
| 3 | Johann Caspar Kerll: *Missa Superba* |
| 4–5 | Jean-Marie Leclair: *Sonatas for Violin and Basso continuo, Opus 5* |
| 6 | *Ten Eighteenth-Century Voluntaries* |
| 7–8 | William Boyce: *Two Anthems for the Georgian Court* |
| 9 | Giulio Caccini: *Le nuove musiche* |
| 10–11 | Jean-Marie Leclair: *Sonatas for Violin and Basso continuo, Opus 9 and Opus 15* |
| 12 | Johann Ernst Eberlin: *Te Deum; Dixit Dominus; Magnificat* |
| 13 | Gregor Aichinger: *Cantiones Ecclesiasticae* |
| 14–15 | Giovanni Legrenzi: *Cantatas and Canzonets for Solo Voice* |
| 16 | Giovanni Francesco Anerio and Francesco Soriano: *Two Settings of Palestrina's "Missa Papae Marcelli"* |
| 17 | Giovanni Paolo Colonna: *Messe a nove voci concertata con stromenti* |
| 18 | Michel Corrette: *"Premier livre d'orgue" and "Nouveau livre de noëls"* |
| 19 | Maurice Greene: *Voluntaries and Suites for Organ and Harpsichord* |
| 20 | Giovanni Antonio Piani: *Sonatas for Violin Solo and Violoncello with Cembalo* |
| 21–22 | Marin Marais: *Six Suites for Viol and Thoroughbass* |
| 23–24 | Dario Castello: *Selected Ensemble Sonatas* |
| 25 | *A Neapolitan Festa a Ballo and Selected Instrumental Ensemble Pieces* |
| 26 | Antonio Vivaldi: *The Manchester Violin Sonatas* |
| 27 | Louis-Nicolas Clérambault: *Two Cantatas for Soprano and Chamber Ensemble* |
| 28 | Giulio Caccini: *Nuove musiche e nuova maniera di scriverle (1614)* |
| 29–30 | Michel Pignolet de Montéclair: *Cantatas for One and Two Voices* |
| 31 | Tomaso Albinoni: *Twelve Cantatas, Opus 4* |
| 32–33 | Antonio Vivaldi: *Cantatas for Solo Voice* |
| 34 | Johann Kuhnau: *Magnificat* |
| 35 | Johann Stadlmayr: *Selected Magnificats* |
| 36–37 | Jacopo Peri: *Euridice: An Opera in One Act, Five Scenes* |
| 38 | Francesco Severi: *Salmi passaggiati (1615)* |
| 39 | George Frideric Handel: *Six Concertos for the Harpsichord or Organ (Walsh's Transcriptions, 1738)* |
| 40 | *The Brasov Tablature (Brasov Music Manuscript 808): German Keyboard Studies 1608–1684* |
| 41 | John Coprario: *Twelve Fantasias for Two Bass Viols and Organ and Eleven Pieces for Three Lyra Viols* |

| | |
|---|---|
| 42 | Antonio Cesti: *Il pomo d'oro (Music for Acts III and V from Modena, Biblioteca Estense, Ms. Mus. E. 120)* |
| 43 | Tomaso Albinoni: *Pimpinone: Intermezzi comici musicali* |
| 44–45 | Antonio Lotti: *Duetti, terzetti, e madrigali a piu voci* |
| 46 | Matthias Weckmann: *Four Sacred Concertos* |
| 47 | Jean Gilles: *Requiem (Messe des morts)* |
| 48 | Marc-Antoine Charpentier: *Vocal Chamber Music* |
| 49 | *Spanish Art Song in the Seventeenth Century* |
| 50 | Jacopo Peri: *"Le varie musiche" and Other Songs* |
| 51–52 | Tomaso Albinoni: *Sonatas and Suites, Opus 8, for Two Violins, Violoncello, and Basso continuo* |
| 53 | Agostino Steffani: *Twelve Chamber Duets* |
| 54–55 | Gregor Aichinger: *The Vocal Concertos* |
| 56 | Giovanni Battista Draghi: *Harpsichord Music* |
| 57 | *Concerted Sacred Music of the Bologna School* |
| 58 | Jean-Marie Leclair: *Sonatas for Violin and Basso continuo, Opus 2* |
| 59 | Isabella Leonarda: *Selected Compositions* |
| 60–61 | Johann Schelle: *Six Chorale Cantatas* |
| 62 | Denis Gaultier: *La Rhétorique des Dieux* |
| 63 | Marc-Antoine Charpentier: *Music for Molière's Comedies* |
| 64–65 | Georg Philipp Telemann: *Don Quichotte auf der Hochzeit des Comacho: Comic Opera-Serenata in One Act* |
| 66 | Henry Butler: *Collected Works* |
| 67–68 | John Jenkins: *The Lyra Viol Consorts* |
| 69 | *Keyboard Transcriptions from the Bach Circle* |
| 70 | Melchior Franck: *Geistliche Gesäng und Melodeyen* |
| 71 | Georg Philipp Telemann: *Douze solos, à violon ou traversière* |
| 72 | Marc-Antoine Charpentier: *Nine Settings of the "Litanies de la Vierge"* |
| 73 | *The Motets of Jacob Praetorius II* |
| 74 | Giovanni Porta: *Selected Sacred Music from the Ospedale della Pietà* |
| 75 | *Fourteen Motets from the Court of Ferdinand II of Hapsburg* |
| 76 | Jean-Marie Leclair: *Sonatas for Violin and Basso continuo, Opus 1* |
| 77 | Antonio Bononcini: *Complete Sonatas for Violoncello and Basso continuo* |
| 78 | Christoph Graupner: *Concerti Grossi for Two Violins* |
| 79 | Paolo Quagliati: *Il primo libro de' madrigali a quattro voci* |
| 80 | Melchior Franck: *Dulces Mundani Exilij Deliciae* |
| 81 | *Late-Seventeenth-Century English Keyboard Music* |
| 82 | *Solo Compositions for Violin and Viola da gamba with Basso continuo* |
| 83 | Barbara Strozzi: *Cantate, ariete a una, due e tre voci, Opus 3* |
| 84 | Charles-Hubert Gervais: *Super flumina Babilonis* |
| 85 | Henry Aldrich: *Selected Anthems and Motet Recompositions* |

| | |
|---|---|
| 86 | Lodovico Grossi da Viadana: *Salmi a quattro cori* |
| 87 | Chiara Margarita Cozzolani: *Motets* |
| 88 | Elisabeth-Claude Jacquet de La Guerre: *Cephale et Procris* |
| 89 | Sébastien Le Camus: *Airs à deux et trois parties* |
| 90 | Thomas Ford: *Lyra Viol Duets* |
| 91 | *Dedication Service for St. Gertrude's Chapel, Hamburg, 1607* |
| 92 | Johann Klemm: *Partitura seu Tabulatura italica* |
| 93 | Giovanni Battista Somis: *Sonatas for Violin and Basso continuo, Opus 3* |
| 94 | John Weldon: *The Judgment of Paris* |
| 95–96 | Juan Bautista Comes: *Masses. Parts 1–2* |
| 97 | Sebastian Knüpfer: *Lustige Madrigalien und Canzonetten* |
| 98 | Stefano Landi: *La morte d'Orfeo* |
| 99 | Giovanni Battista Fontana: *Sonatas for One, Two, and Three Parts with Basso continuo* |
| 100 | Georg Philipp Telemann: *Twelve Trios* |
| 101 | Fortunato Chelleri: *Keyboard Music* |
| 102 | Johann David Heinichen: *La gara degli Dei* |
| 103 | Johann David Heinichen: *Diana su l'Elba* |
| 104 | Alessandro Scarlatti: *Venere, Amore e Ragione* |
| 105 | *Songs with Theorbo (ca. 1650–1663)* |
| 106 | Melchior Franck: *Paradisus Musicus* |
| 107 | Heinrich Ignaz Franz von Biber: *Missa Christi resurgentis* |
| 108 | Johann Ludwig Bach: *Motets* |
| 109–10 | Giovanni Rovetta: *Messa, e salmi concertati, op. 4 (1639). Parts 1–2* |
| 111 | Johann Joachim Quantz: *Seven Trio Sonatas* |
| 112 | *Petits motets from the Royal Convent School at Saint-Cyr* |
| 113 | Isabella Leonarda: *Twelve Sonatas, Opus 16* |
| 114 | Rudolph di Lasso: *Virginalia Eucharistica (1615)* |
| 115 | Giuseppe Torelli: *Concerti musicali, Opus 6* |
| 116–17 | Nicola Francesco Haym: *Complete Sonatas. Parts 1–2* |
| 118 | Benedetto Marcello: *Il pianto e il riso delle quattro stagioni* |
| 119 | Loreto Vittori: *La Galatea* |
| 120–23 | William Lawes: *Collected Vocal Music. Parts 1–4* |
| 124 | Marco da Gagliano: *Madrigals. Part 1* |
| 125 | Johann Schop: *Erster Theil newer Paduanen* |
| 126 | Giovanni Felice Sances: *Motetti a una, due, tre, e quattro voci (1638)* |
| 127 | Thomas Elsbeth: *Sontägliche Evangelien* |
| 128–30 | Giovanni Antonio Rigatti: *Messa e salmi, parte concertati. Parts 1–3* |
| 131 | *Seventeenth-Century Lutheran Church Music with Trombones* |
| 132 | Francesco Cavalli: *La Doriclea* |
| 133 | *Music for "Macbeth"* |

| | |
|---|---|
| 134 | Domenico Allegri: *Music for an Academic Defense (Rome, 1617)* |
| 135 | Jean Gilles: *Diligam te, Domine* |
| 136 | Silvius Leopold Weiss: *Lute Concerti* |
| 137 | *Masses by Alessandro Scarlatti and Francesco Gasparini* |
| 138 | Giovanni Ghizzolo: *Madrigali et arie per sonare et cantare* |
| 139 | Michel Lambert: *Airs from "Airs de différents autheurs"* |
| 140 | William Babell: *Twelve Solos for a Violin or Oboe with Basso Continuo. Book 1* |
| 141 | Giovanni Francesco Anerio: *Selva armonica (Rome, 1617)* |
| 142–43 | Bellerofonte Castaldi: *Capricci (1622). Parts 1–2* |
| 144 | Georg von Bertouch: *Sonatas a 3* |
| 145 | Marco da Gagliano: *Madrigals. Part 2* |
| 146 | Giovanni Rovetta: *Masses* |
| 147 | Giacomo Antonio Perti: *Five-Voice Motets for the Assumption of the Virgin Mary* |
| 148 | Giovanni Felice Sances: *Motetti a 2, 3, 4, e cinque voci (1642)* |
| 149 | *La grand-mére amoureuse, parodie d'Atys* |
| 150 | Andreas Hammerschmidt: *Geistlicher Dialogen Ander Theil* |
| 151 | Georg von Bertouch: *Three Sacred Cantatas* |
| 152 | Giovanni Maria Ruggieri: *Two Settings of the Gloria* |
| 153 | Alessandro Scarlatti: *Concerti sacri, opera seconda* |
| 154 | Johann Sigismund Kusser: *Adonis* |
| 155 | John Blow: *Selected Verse Anthems* |
| 156 | Anton Holzner: *Viretum pierium (1621)* |
| 157 | Alessandro Scarlatti: *Venere, Adone, et Amore* |
| 158 | Marc-Antoine Charpentier: *In nativitatem Domini canticum, H. 416* |
| 159 | Francesco Scarlatti: *Six Concerti Grossi* |
| 160 | Charles Avison: *Concerto Grosso Arrangements of Geminiani's Opus 1 Violin Sonatas* |
| 161 | Johann David Heinichen: *Selected Music for Vespers* |
| 162–63 | Francesco Gasparini: *Cantatas with Violins. Parts 1–2* |
| 164–65 | Antoine Boesset: *Sacred Music. Parts 1–2* |
| 166 | Andreas Hammerschmidt: *Selections from the "Gespräche" (1655–56) with Capellen* |
| 167 | Santiago de Murcia: *Cifras selectas de guitarra* |
| 168 | Gottfried Heinrich Stölzel: *German Te Deum* |
| 169 | Biagio Marini: *Compositioni varie per musica di camera, Opus 13* |
| 170 | Santiago Billoni: *Complete Works* |
| 171 | Marco da Gagliano: *La Flora* |
| 172 | Girolamo Polani: *Six Chamber Cantatas for Solo Voice* |
| 173 | Bonifazio Graziani: *Motets for Two to Six Voices, Opus 1* |
| 174 | Marco da Gagliano: *Madrigals. Part 3* |
| 175 | Alessandro Scarlatti: *Solo Serenatas* |
| 176 | John Eccles: *Rinaldo and Armida* |

177    Tarquinio Merula: *Curtio precipitato et altri capricii (1638)*
178    *Jean Racine's* Cantiques spirituels
179    Antonio Rodríguez Mata: *Passions*
180    Philippe Courbois: *Cantatas for One and Two Voices*
181    Alessandro Scarlatti: *Selected Sacred Music*